Adele Welsby's
Cross Stitch
Characters

David & Charles

To all the contributors involved with this book, and all their wonderful characters

A DAVID & CHARLES BOOK

First published in the UK in 2002

ISBN 0 7153 1206 5

Executive editor Cheryl Brown
Executive art editor Ali Myer
Designer Lisa Forrester
Project editing and chart manipulation Linda Clements
Photography Lucy Mason
Printed and bound in the UK by Butler & Tanner Ltd, Frome and London

David & Charles
Brunel House   Newton Abbot   Devon

CONTENTS

INTRODUCTION

Classic character illustrations are the inspiration for this varied collection of cross stitch designs – and a wonderful selection there is too, with projects suitable for the whole family to stitch and enjoy.

Wallace and Gromit, the famous duo, are household names and personal favourites of mine. I was thrilled to visit the studios at Aardman Animations where I was able to admire their many trophies and see a little of the work that goes on behind the scenes. The cheese-loving inventor and his long-suffering dog feature in some wonderful, fun designs and unusual projects which are sure to appeal to everyone.

Mr Men and Little Miss were created over thirty years ago and still maintain their fresh appeal. I am delighted to include them in the book as everyone can identify with a Mr Happy or a Little Miss Chatterbox, as I know only too well having a daughter, Laura, who is just like Little Miss Splendid, Little Miss Chatterbox and Little Miss Bossy all rolled into one! These designs are bright and simple and ideal for someone just starting cross stitch.

Children could stitch them on a large count Aida.

I have a special relationship with Percy the Park Keeper as I have been designing and producing cross stitch kits about him for several years. Percy tends to his park whilst being a good friend to the animals who often need his help. The designs included are from the many book illustrations and require a backstitch and long stitch outline, which makes them suitable for a

more skilled stitcher.

I adore the mice who live at the bottom of Brambly Hedge and am really happy that these well known classic stories, painted in gentle watercolours in Jill Barklem's charming books, are included in my book. To represent the original illustrations as faithfully as possible, the designs use fractional stitches and are ideal for the more experienced stitcher.

Harry and the Bucketful of Dinosaurs, a modern-day story, is an endearing and charming tale of a little boy and his discovery of dinosaurs. It reminds me of the fun I had with my son, Matthew, who also loved dinosaurs. The lively designs are full of colourful detail and are outlined in backstitch and long stitch. The Large Family from Jill Murphy's *Five Minutes' Peace* completes the line-up of characters. These cheerful elephants are just a delight and I can identify with Mrs Large as I am sure any mother can – what would we all give for five minutes' peace! The original illustrations are bright and colourful and reflecting that in the designs requires some fractional stitches and backstitch outlines.

I have made up the designs into many attractive finished projects, some simple others a little more complicated. There are also many suggestions and ideas throughout the book for other uses which are sure to appeal to adults and children alike and to suit stitchers of all levels of ability. I hope some of my favourite characters are also yours. Enjoy the stitching!

THE LARGE FAMILY

The Large family, created by Jill Murphy, tells of the trials and tribulations of everyday life through the eyes of a family of elephants. In *Five Minutes' Peace*, Mrs Large, like any overworked mother, just wants a little time to herself. However, Lester, Laura and the baby have other ideas.

The Large family is just like any family – messy, noisy and of course nosey. The elephants have human characteristics which are warm and amusing and are a delight to children and adults alike. Jill Murphy describes in words and pictures a typical morning in a family home. Breakfast is a devastating sight and, understandably, Mrs Large wants to escape from it to have a bath but the children inevitably follow, catch her and we can all imagine what happens then.

The designs in this chapter are very adaptable and you can use them for many different projects. Baby Large, wearing his breakfast, would make a lovely patch on clothing or, as seen here, as a placemat. Mrs Large, snoozing in the bath, has been made into a fantastic neck pillow – an essential item for a long soak. Keeping writing and drawing clutter tidy is easy with a pencil case featuring the Large children chasing after their mother who only wants five minutes peace.

Baby Large Placemat

Baby Large looks terrific on the front of a really useful placemat (see photograph on previous page). The design has been created by stitching the main motif with a framing border, and personalized by adding a name using the alphabet chart from page 54.

STITCHING IDEAS

To keep the stitching clean, after you have added the interfacing take the work to a printer and ask them to laminate it. This design would also look wonderful made into a cushion with a fringed edge.

STITCH COUNT
105 x 105

DESIGN SIZE
19 x 19cm (7½ x 7½in)
approx

WHAT YOU NEED

27 x 27cm (10½ x 10½in)
snow blue 14 count
Aida (Fabric Flair
N14.550)

DMC stranded cotton
(floss) as in chart key

Tapestry needle

27 x 27cm (10½ x 10½in)
medium-weight
interfacing

27 x 27cm (10½ x 10½in)
backing fabric

Matching sewing thread

1 Prepare your fabric for work (see Techniques). Use two strands of stranded cotton (floss) for cross stitch and one strand for backstitching, outlining and French knot for the eye. Begin by stitching the border 3.5cm (1½in) up and in from the corner of the fabric to form a 19cm (7½in) square. Now stitch Baby Large. Finally, you can personalize the design by adding a name using the alphabet on page 54, or any of the alphabets in the book. When stitching is complete press the work carefully.

2 To make the placemat, place the embroidered fabric right side down and taking the piece of interfacing, press it onto the fabric with a damp cloth. This will help to stiffen the embroidery.

3 Pin the backing fabric and embroidered fabric together with right sides facing. Allowing a 1cm (½in) seam allowance, sew around all the edges leaving a small gap on one side. Turn through to the right side and slipstitch the gap closed, then press gently.

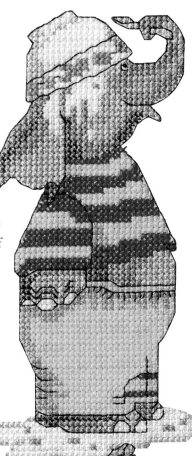

STITCHING IDEAS

This design would look great as a patch on a T-shirt or other garment. The patch could be neatly sewn on with the edges hemmed or it could be bound with bias binding before being sewn on. For a rustic effect, fray the edges of the embroidery fabric and then fuse the patch to the clothing using Bondaweb. As an alternative, the patch would look wonderful as a pocket on a pair of dungarees – in which case only three sides would be sewn to the garment. You could add contrasting bias binding or ric-rac braid as an edging to the top of the pocket.

BABY LARGE PLACEMAT KEY

DMC stranded cotton

Cross stitch

224	
318	
340	
414	
415	
444	
519	
606	
676	
783	
900	
906	
928	
970	
3820	
B5200	

Backstitch
3799

French knot
3799

Name space

Large Family Pencil Case

Mrs Large has made her escape from her children. She has asked them to play downstairs whilst she has a much earned bath. However, the children have other ideas and set off to join her in one of their favourite pastimes. The delightful design on a useful pencil case (see page 9) shows them following their mother.

(see page 9)

STITCHING IDEA

Why not stitch Baby Large's teddy bear on 14 count fabric to fit a fun clip for holding paintings or stories? (See picture below and chart on page 14.) Follow the manufacturer's instructions to fit the embroidery into the recessed fun clip front. Fix in place using glue or double-sided tape.

STITCH COUNT
142 x 76

DESIGN SIZE
25 x 13.5cm (10 x 5⅓in) approx

WHAT YOU NEED

Two pieces 33 x 18cm (13 x 7in) snow blue 14 count Aida (Fabric Flair N14.550)

●

DMC stranded cotton (floss) as in chart key

●

Tapestry needle

●

Two pieces 33 x 18cm (13 x 7in) lining material

●

30cm (12in) zip

1 Prepare your fabric for work and mark the centre (see Techniques). Begin stitching from the centre following the chart overleaf, using two strands of stranded cotton (floss) for cross stitching and one strand for backstitching, outlining and French knots. When stitching is complete press the work carefully.

2 To make the pencil case, pin one side of the zip on the front of the embroidered fabric from the wrong side and then pin the lining fabric on the other side of the zip. Machine stitch in place then remove the pins. Open the zip and repeat for the two remaining pieces of fabric.

3 Turn the fabric through so that right sides are together. Hem down the short sides and then along the bottom of the case. Trim the corners and neaten the edges, turn through to the right side, pushing out the corners, and your pencil case is ready for use.

Ruler

A simple cross stitch border can be used to enhance many designs. Here, the simple border pattern from Baby Large's Placemat chart on page 11 is used to decorate a ruler – simply stitch a sufficient length of the border to fit (see Suppliers, page 111).

(see Suppliers, page 111).

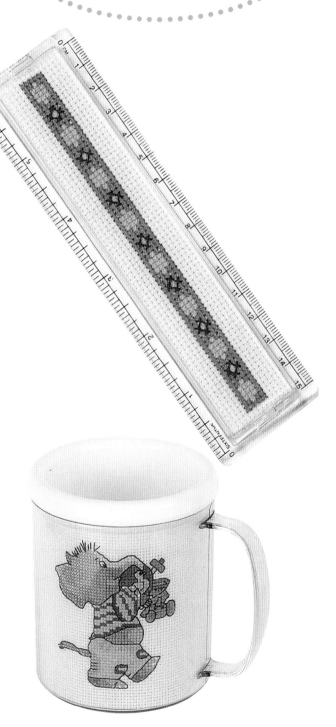

STITCH COUNT

5 x 77

DESIGN SIZE

1 x 14cm (⅜ x 5½in) approx

WHAT YOU NEED

16.5 x 5cm (6½ x 2in) snow blue 14 count Aida (Fabric Flair N14.550)

DMC stranded cotton (floss) as in chart key

Tapestry needle

Ruler (Framecraft)

Iron-on interfacing

1 Prepare your fabric for work and mark the centre (see Techniques). Begin stitching from the centre following the placemat border charted on page 11. Use two strands for cross stitching.

2 Cut a length of interfacing to the size of the embroidered fabric, then follow the manufacturer's instructions to iron it on to the back of the embroidery.

3 Trim the fabric to the size of the ruler aperture, place in the aperture, right side up, and close the top.

STITCHING IDEA

Stitching only Baby Large from the chart on page 14 would be a perfect decoration for a baby's mug. Stitch on 18 count fabric to reduce the size, back with iron-on interfacing and place inside the mug following the manufacturer's instructions.

LARGE FAMILY PENCIL CASE KEY

DMC stranded cotton

Cross stitch

208	606	721
301	646	762
318	647	781
452	648	783

799	973	3821
906	3072	3825
956	3799	B5200
957	3801	

Backstitch/Long stitch

726

3799

French knots

- 318
- 606
- 3799

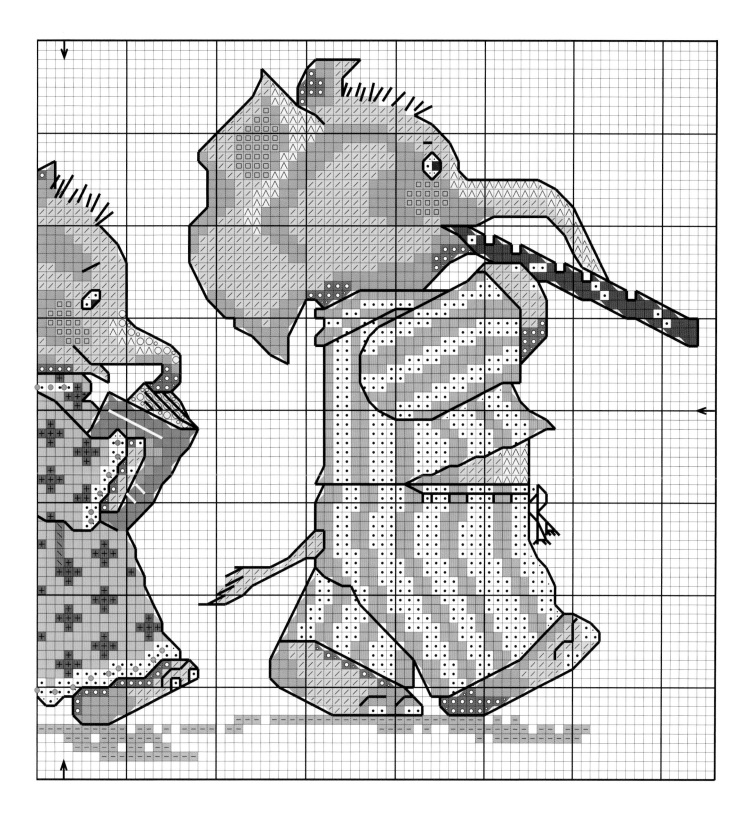

Mrs Large's Bath Cushion

Mrs Large has at last managed to slip away from her children and has run a lovely hot bath in which she is enjoying a long soak, or so she believes. Five minutes peace doesn't seem too much to ask for but children usually have other ideas. This design has been used on the cover of a blow-up neck cushion – an essential item for a long, relaxing soak!

STITCH COUNT
89 x 73

DESIGN SIZE
16 x 13cm (6½ x 5¼in) approx

WHAT YOU NEED

19 x 17cm (7½ x 6½in) cream 28 count Jobelan (Fabric Flair NJ429.10)

DMC stranded cotton (floss) as in chart key

Tapestry needle

16 x 13cm (6½ x 5in) Bondaweb

43 x 30cm (17 x 12in) yellow fleece

Two pieces 43 x 19cm (17 x 7½in) green fleece

Two pieces 28 x 20cm (11 x 8in) green fleece

Blow-up neck cushion (available through chemists)

1 Prepare your fabric for work and mark the centre (see Techniques). Begin stitching from the centre over two fabric threads, following the chart. Use two strands of stranded cotton (floss) for cross stitching and one strand for backstitching and outlining. When stitching is complete press carefully.

2 To make the bath cushion, cut a piece of Bondaweb 16 x 13cm (6½ x 5in) and dry iron it, adhesive side down, centrally onto the wrong side of the embroidery. Now place the embroidered piece centrally on the piece of yellow fleece, right side up. Cover with a damp cloth and press with a hot, dry iron to fuse together. Once cool, fray the edges of the stitched piece (see photograph).

3 Pin the 28 x 20cm (11 x 8in) rectangles of green fleece to the short ends of the yellow fleece, with raw edges matching and tack (baste) together. These pieces will be cut and knotted later.

4 To make the cushions backs, take the two 43 x 19cm (17 x 7½in) green fleece rectangles and fold over and stitch 1cm (½in) of each long edge to make a hem. Place the cushion backs on the cushion front with right sides facing. Stitch along the edges of the cushion, then trim the corners and turn right side out. On either short edge of the cushion will be a rectangle of green fleece. Cut the fleece into eight strips stopping 1cm (½in) from the edge of the yellow fleece. Tie these strips into knots for a novel finish.

5 Blow up the pillow and insert into the cushion, which leaves you with the pleasure of a long soak after all that hard work. Enjoy!

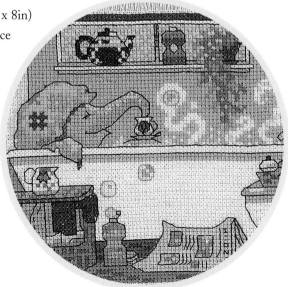

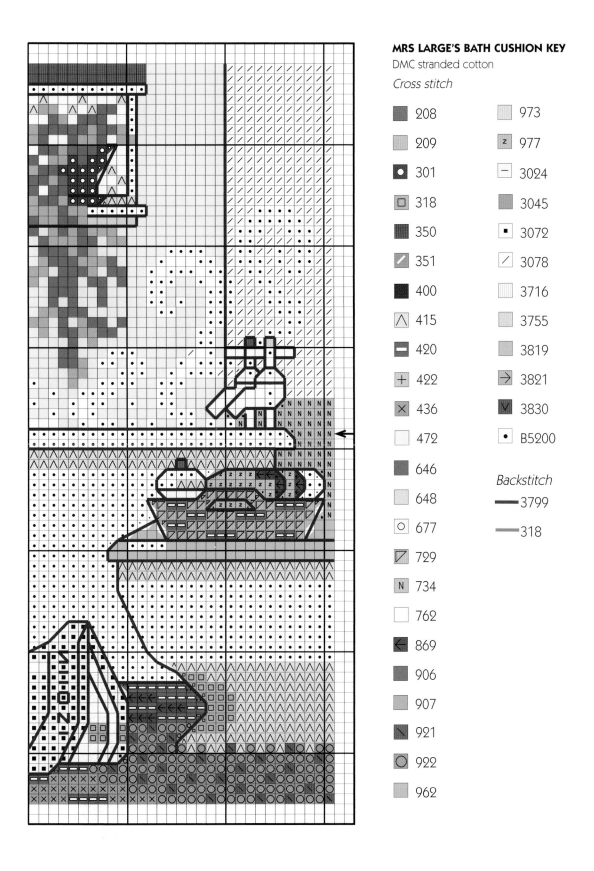

Cross stitch

208		973	
209		z	977
◖	301	−	3024
▢	318		3045
350		▪	3072
╱	351	╱	3078
400			3716
∧	415		3755
▬	420		3819
+	422	→	3821
✕	436	Ⅴ	3830
	472	•	B5200
646			
648			
○	677		

Backstitch

▨	729
N	734
	762
←	869
906	
907	
◣	921
○	922
962	

Backstitch

▬▬ 3799

▬▬ 318

BRAMBLY HEDGE™

Jill Barklem's series of books about the mice of Brambly Hedge are a delight and a fruitful source of cross stitch inspiration as this chapter shows. Brambly Hedge is on the other side of the stream, across the field. The hedge is made from elderberry and hawthorn bushes, brambles, wild roses, ferns, violets and trails of honeysuckle. At its centre is a large, ivy-covered tree stump and if you look closely you will see small front doors half hidden in tangled roots – entrances to the homes of the mice who inhabit the hedge.

The mice who live in the caring community of Brambly Hedge are in harmony with their environment and are able to obtain everything they need for their daily lives from the hedgerow and fields around them. They work very hard – getting up early when the dew is still on the grass in order to pick fresh fruits, nuts and flowers. Although they work hard, the mice still have time for plenty of fun. They love an excuse for a celebration and no birthday, wedding or anniversary goes by unnoticed.

Young Wilfred Toadflax's surprise birthday party is the theme in *Spring Story* and inspired me to create a naming sampler to celebrate a new arrival. His best friend and fellow adventurer, Primrose Woodmouse, features in a versatile night case, showing an exhausted Primrose fast asleep after her adventures in *Autumn Story*. *Summer Story* tells the tale of Dusty Dogwood's and Poppy Eyebright's wedding, this event featuring on the lid of a trousseau box for keeping special wedding mementos. There is also a pretty ring cushion on the same theme.

Forever and ever

Charlotte and Matthew
18th July 2004

Poppy's Trousseau Box

In *Summer Story*, midsummer's day sees Poppy Eyebright marry Dusty Dogwood on the stream, the coolest and quite the most romantic of places. This charming design of the couple pronounced mouse and wife has been made up into a lovely pine trousseau box, perfect for all those precious wedding mementos (shown on page 21).

STITCHING IDEAS

This is such a pretty design, it would delight a newly married couple if framed attractively, ready to hang on a wall.

STITCH COUNT
100 x 79 (with names and dates)

DESIGN SIZE
18 x 14cm (7 x 5½in) approx

WHAT YOU NEED

20 x 20cm (8 x 8in) English rose 28 count Jobelan (Fabric Flair NJ429.167)

●

DMC stranded cotton (floss) as in chart key

Tapestry needle

●

24 x 24cm (9½ x 9½in) pine box (see Suppliers) spray painted a pearly apricot

Card insert slightly larger than box aperture

Polyester wadding (batting)

●

Strong sewing thread

1 Prepare your fabric for work and mark the centre (see Techniques). Begin stitching the Poppy and Dusty part of the design from the centre over two fabric threads following the chart overleaf. Use two strands of stranded cotton (floss) for cross stitching and one strand for backstitching and outlining. When stitching is complete press the work carefully.

2 To personalize the design, plot the names and dates you wish to use on graph paper (see page 105) to ensure they fit the space available (marked with dotted lines on the chart). Use the alphabet and numbers charted on page 23 and work with one strand in backstitch and French knots using DMC 3799, or a colour of your choice.

3 To mount in a box, place a square of wadding (batting) on to the card insert for the lid. Carefully fold your stitching over the top and check that it will fit into the box lid. You may have to trim the card and wadding (batting). Mount the embroidery on to the card by laying the stitching face down and placing the wadding and card centrally over it. Pin the embroidery at the centre of each side and add a few more pins either side of these. Lace across the back of the embroidery with strong sewing thread and then remove the pins. Place the embroidery in the recess of the box lid, then replace the board backing and fold-in fasteners to secure the back firmly in place.

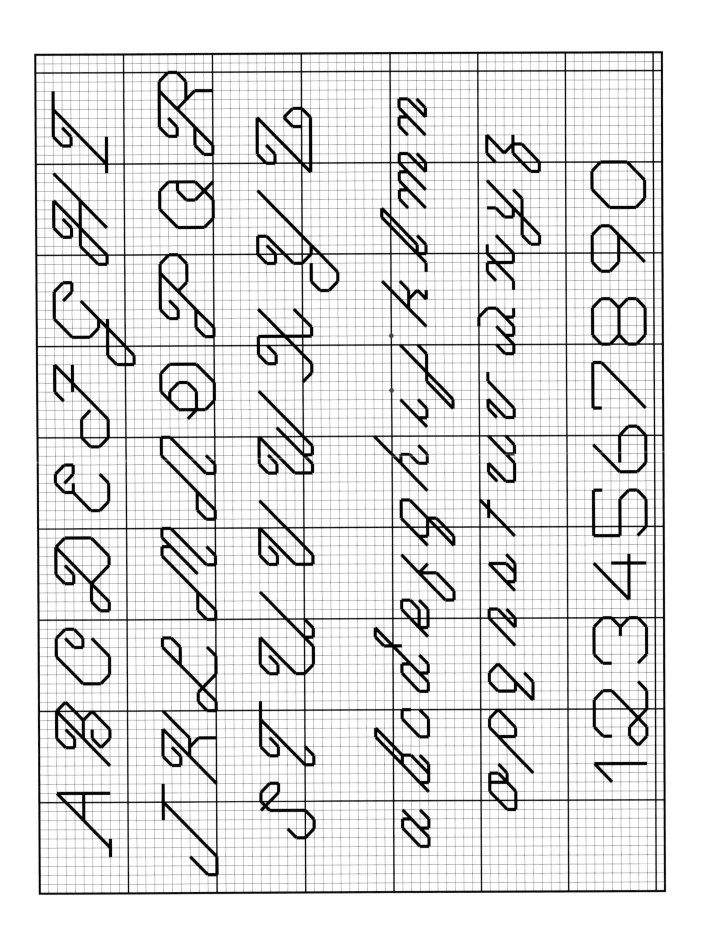

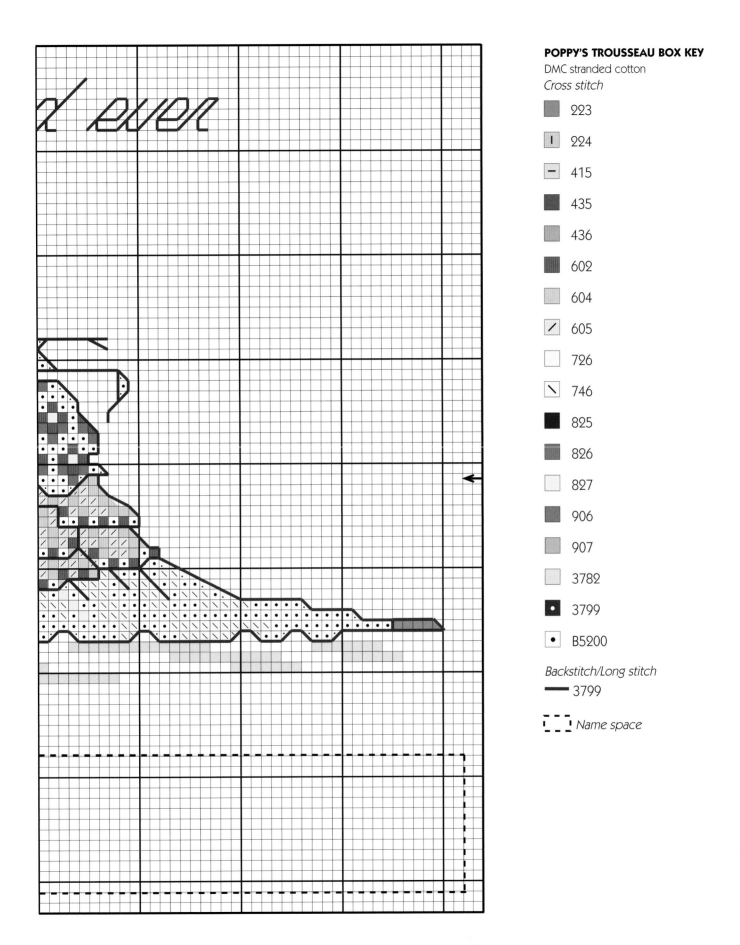

POPPY'S TROUSSEAU BOX KEY
DMC stranded cotton
Cross stitch

▨	223
I	224
–	415
▨	435
▨	436
▨	602
▨	604
╱	605
☐	726
╲	746
■	825
▨	826
☐	827
▨	906
▨	907
☐	3782
⊡	3799
•	B5200

Backstitch/Long stitch
━━ 3799

⌐ ¬ Name space
└ ┘

Forever and Ever Cushion

A charming ring cushion features an adapted design from Poppy's Trousseau Box. It is very quick and simple to stitch and with the addition of some heart-shaped buttons and a little lace is turned into a lovely memento.

STITCH COUNT

64 x 62

DESIGN SIZE

11.5 x 11.5cm (4½ x 4⅛in) approx

WHAT YOU NEED

15 x 15cm (6 x 6in) English rose 28 count Jobelan (Fabric Flair NJ429.167)

DMC stranded cotton (floss) as in chart key

Four Mill Hill maroon heart-shaped buttons (Framecraft)

15 x 15cm (6 x 6in) backing fabric

1m (40in) x 2.5cm (1in) wide lace

Matching sewing thread

Polyester wadding (batting)

Pair of rings (Framecraft)

50cm (20in) each maroon and cream ribbons

1. Prepare your fabric for work and mark the centre (see Techniques). Begin stitching from the centre over two fabric threads following the chart. Use two strands of stranded cotton for cross stitching and one for back-stitching. With matching sewing thread, sew the heart buttons on in each inner corner (see photograph below).

2. To make the cushion, pin and tack (baste) the lace all around the edge of the embroidery on the right side. Remove the pins, then fold over the short lace ends and sew together neatly.

3. Pin the backing fabric on top of the lace and machine stitch around the cushion 1cm (½in) from the edge, leaving a small gap at one side. Turn through to the right side. Fill with wadding (batting) and slipstitch the gap to close. Tie a bow with the maroon and cream ribbons and sew in the centre of the cushion together with the rings.

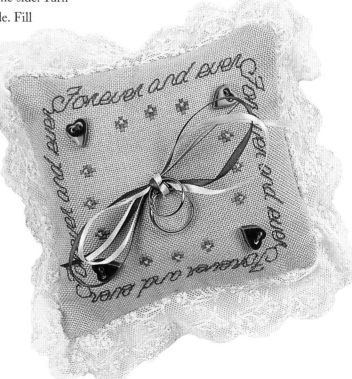

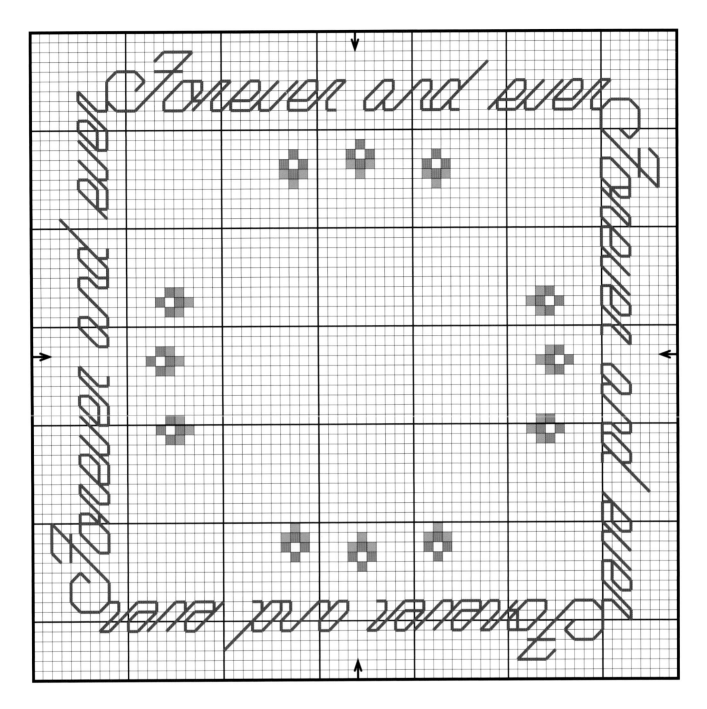

FOREVER AND EVER CUSHION KEY

. DMC stranded cotton

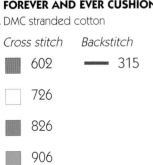

Cross stitch	*Backstitch*
602	315
726	
826	
906	

Naming Sampler

As the sun begins to sink in Jill Barklem's *Spring Story*, an exhausted but happy Wilfred Toadflax is wheeled home after his wonderful surprise birthday party. The story was the inspiration behind this pretty naming sampler which features Wilfred asleep in a wheelbarrow. The sampler would be perfect to celebrate any child's birth – simply use the alphabet chart provided to change the name.

STITCH COUNT
153 x 117

DESIGN SIZE
28 x 21.5cm (11 x 8½in) approx

WHAT YOU NEED

36 x 29cm (14 x 11½in) forget-me-not blue 28 count Jobelan (Fabric Flair NJ429.103)

●

DMC stranded cotton (floss) as in chart key

●

Tapestry needle

1 Prepare your fabric for work and mark the centre (see Techniques). Begin stitching from the centre over two fabric threads following the chart overleaf. Use two strands of stranded cotton (floss) for cross stitching and one strand for backstitching, outlining and French knots.

2 Stitch the name of your choice within the dotted lines on the chart, using the alphabet charted on page 32. I have used a pink (602) but the colour can be of your choice. It would be advisable to plan the name on graph paper before stitching (see page 105).

3 When all stitching is complete, press your embroidery carefully and then frame the work.

the hill comes the rising sun
on the fields, and on you.
...ne.

CHARLOTTE

And over the hill come
To shine on the field
little one.

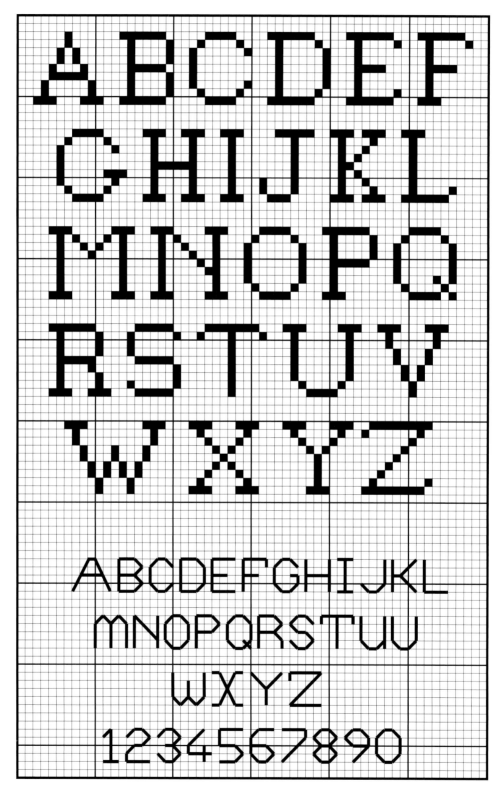

NAMING SAMPLER ALPHABET

Stitch the bricks from the top of the Naming Sampler on to a ready-made bib spelling a child's name from the alphabet given opposite. A block stitched on to a piece of towelling using waste canvas with a letter T stitched in the centre looks lovely in a small ceramic pot lid ready for the tooth fairy's visit (see below). Alternatively, any letter could be embroidered on Aida for a pot lid, using one of the alphabet charts.

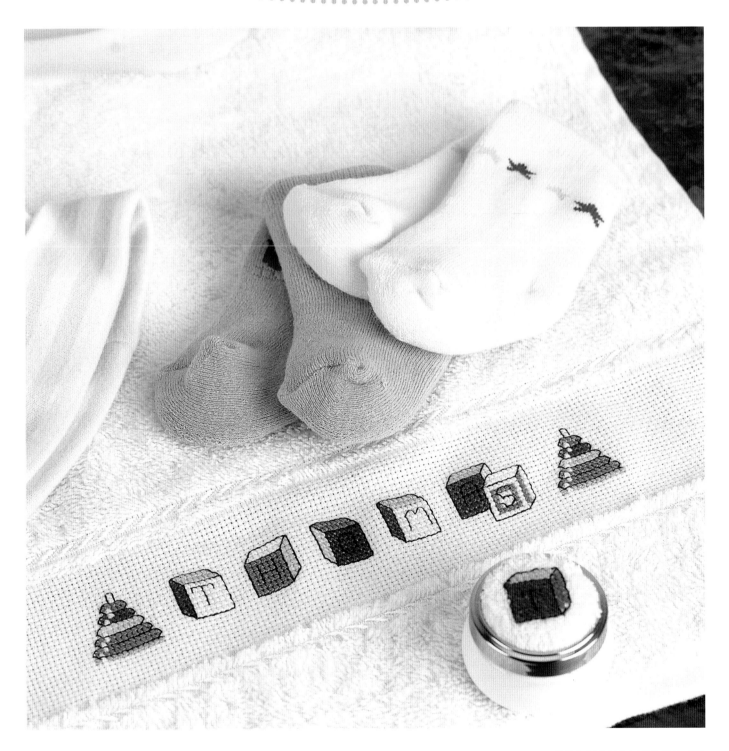

Primrose's Night Case

This lovely design is taken from Jill Barklem's *Autumn Story*, one of her delightful chronicles of life in the hedgerows. In this harvest-time adventure, Primrose meets some harvest mice but then gets lost in the wood. This pretty night case shows Primrose snuggled under her colourful quilt, dreaming of the next adventure.

STITCH COUNT
136 x 118

DESIGN SIZE
25 x 21cm (9¾ x 8½in) approx

WHAT YOU NEED

1m x 56cm (40 x 22in) honeysuckle pink 28 count Jobelan (Fabric Flair NJ429.102)

DMC stranded cotton (floss) as in chart key

Tapestry needle

1m x 56cm (40 x 22in) white satin lining fabric

Matching sewing thread

1 Prepare you fabric for work (see Techniques). Begin stitching 7.5cm (3in) from one short edge of the fabric. Stitch over two threads of the fabric following the chart overleaf, using two strands of stranded cotton (floss) for cross stitching and French knots and one strand for backstitching and outlining. Once the stitching is complete press the embroidery carefully.

2 To make up the night case, place the satin lining and embroidery right sides facing and pin and tack (baste) together. With the embroidered piece upwards, machine stitch around the edge taking a small seam allowance and leaving a small gap for turning.

3 Cut across the corners and trim the seam to reduce bulk. Turn through to the right side, easing out the corners. Slipstitch the gap to close. Fold the panel in three, then neatly oversew the side seams to finish the case.

STITCHING IDEAS

This night case could be made into a pillowcase by simply attaching satin ribbon ties or a strip of Velcro to fasten the front flap.

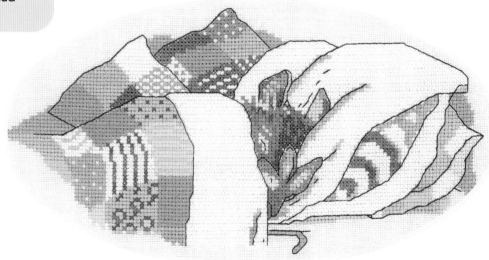

Ease Your whiskers, rest your paws.
Pies and puddings fill the stores.
Sweetly dream the night away
Till sunshine brings another day

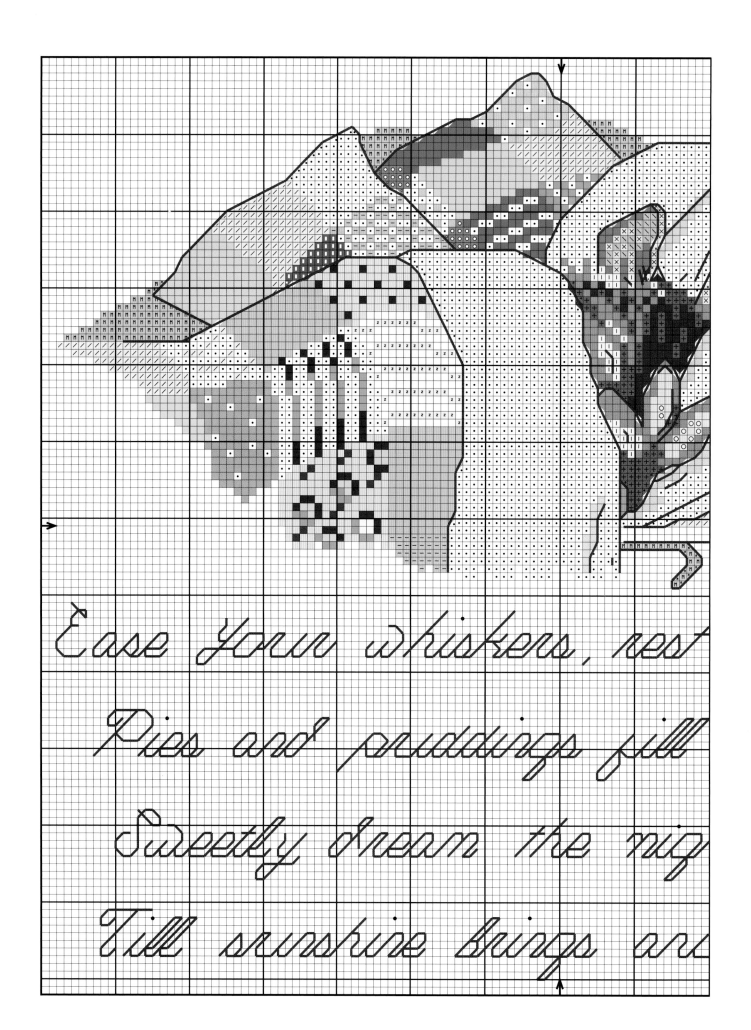

Ease Your whiskers, rest

Pies and puddings fill

Sweetly dream the nig

Till sunshine brings an

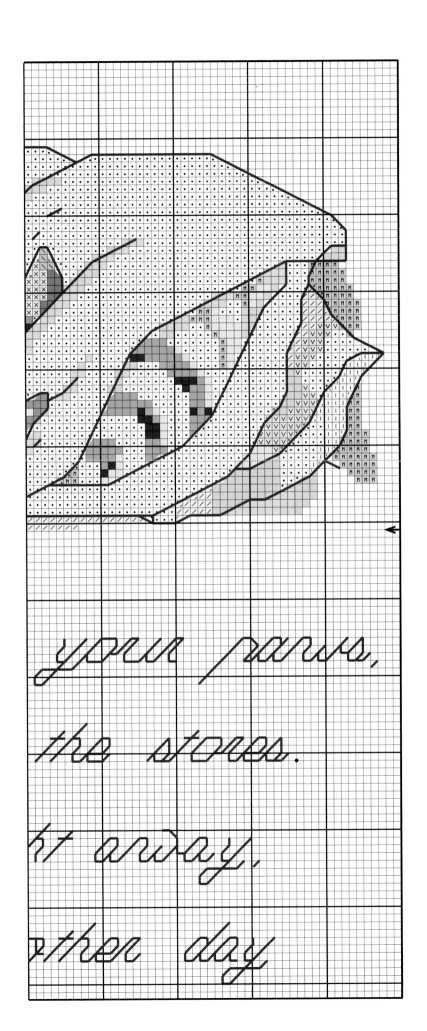

DMC stranded cotton

Cross stitch

■	223	░	605
\	224	z	726
×	225	I	746
▨	307	▨	813
▨	402	O	819
▨	415	■	826
■	434	/	827
+	435	■	904
▨	436	V	928
□	445	M	3354
◉	518	−	3755
▨	563	▨	3810
■	602	▨	3819
▨	603	•	B5200

Backstitch
— 3799

French knots
● 3799

Dreamy Star Cushions

The poem from *Autumn Story* used on the night case has been adapted to create two smaller designs. These have been stitched as panels on two star-shaped cushions, which will look very inviting lying on your pillow. The designs would also make lovely framed pictures.

STITCH COUNTS
56 x 19 and 67 x 19

DESIGN SIZES
10 x 3.5cm (4 x 1¼in) and
12 x 3.5cm (4¾ x 1¼in) approx

WHAT YOU NEED

Two pieces 10 x 15cm (4 x 6in)
honeysuckle pink 28 count Jobelan
(Fabric Flair NJ429.102)

DMC stranded cotton (floss) 602

Tapestry needle

½m (½yd) each pink and
yellow gingham

Bondaweb

Polyester wadding (batting)

Eight self-cover buttons

Matching sewing thread

1 Prepare your fabric for work and mark the centre (see Techniques). Stitch from the centre over two fabric threads following the charts (right), using one strand of DMC 602 (pink) stranded cotton (floss) for backstitching and French knots.

2 To make up the cushions, enlarge the star shape here on a photocopier to 300%, or until the dotted centre line measures 17.5cm (7in). Use this as a pattern to cut two stars each from the yellow and pink gingham.

3 To make the yellow star, cut a rectangle of Bondaweb 2.5cm (1in) smaller than the embroidered piece. Place the Bondaweb centrally on the back of the embroidery, leaving a border around the edge and iron into place. Fringe the embroidery around the four unbonded sides and, with right side up, iron the embroidery on to one piece of yellow gingham, following the manufacturer's instructions.

4 Pin the front and back pieces of yellow gingham together with right sides facing. Machine stitch around the edges taking a small seam allowance and leaving a small gap for turning. Trim the seam and the corners to reduce bulk and turn right side out. Stuff with polyester wadding (batting) and slipstitch the opening to close.

5 Cover four of the self-cover buttons with scraps of yellow gingham following the manufacturer's instructions, then stitch the buttons on the corners of the embroidered design. To make a pink gingham star, follow steps 3–5.

Star template

Enlarge star template on a photocopier by 300% or until dotted line measures 17.5cm (7in).

Sweetly dream the night away

Till sunshine brings another day

PERCY THE PARK KEEPER

Percy the Park Keeper is the wonderful creation of Nick Butterworth. Percy, a kindly and fun-loving character, first appeared in the much loved illustrated books but he now also appears in animated films shown on television and video.

Percy loves to spend time with his animal friends, even though his work in the park keeps him very busy. The animals often need Percy to lend a helping hand when there is some little crisis to deal with, usually concerning a fox or a badger, a mole or a mouse. There is always plenty to do in the park but Percy likes a bit of fun and mischief too and there is nothing he enjoys more than a picnic.

I have used individual characters from many of Nick Butterworth's books, including *After the Storm, The Secret Path* and *A Bumpy Ride*. These classic tales have been brought to life in cross stitch in this chapter beginning with a delightful birth sampler featuring many of the animals, where, as usual, badger is up to mischief. Percy, resting on a wall with his animal friends, is mounted as a charming picture and there is also an art folder (pictured here) showing Percy from *A Bumpy Ride* with his latest invention, a special lawn-mower.

Percy's Art Folder

In *A Bumpy Ride*, Percy is busy for three whole days. As his animal friends try to guess what he is making, he suddenly emerges sitting on top of a very strange machine. He has made his own special lawn-mower, which takes them on a very bumpy ride. A lovely art folder complements this exciting design.

STITCH COUNT

120 x 112

DESIGN SIZE

22 x 20cm (8½ x 8in) approx

WHAT YOU NEED

30 x 30cm (12 x 12in) cream
14 count Aida

DMC stranded cotton (floss) as in
chart key

Tapestry needle

32 x 64cm (12½ x 25in) yellow
corrugated card

30 x 30cm (12 x 12in) backing card

Double-sided adhesive tape

Masking tape

60cm (24in) green cord

1 Prepare your fabric for work and mark the centre (see Techniques). Begin stitching from the centre following the charts on pages 44–47. Use two strands of stranded cotton (floss) for cross stitching and one strand for backstitching, outlining, long stitches and French knots.

2 To make the folder, fold the yellow corrugated card in half lengthways. Using a craft knife cut a window 22 x 22cm (8½ x 8½in) out of the centre of one half. Stick double-sided tape all around the inside of the window.

STITCHING IDEAS

This fun design could just as easily be framed as a picture or placed in the front of a box lid or made into a pretty cushion.

3 Trim the embroidery to within 2.5cm (1in) of the stitching. Mount the embroidery onto the backing card using double-sided tape. With the embroidery facing up, place the window centrally over it and press it down on to the double-sided tape. Neaten the back of the window using masking tape. Lastly, make two holes at the top of the folder with a hole punch, thread the green cord through and knot the ends.

STITCHING IDEA

A triangular pencil pot (see Suppliers) makes a good partner to the art folder. The photograph (right) shows that it uses an amusing part of the Birth Sampler (chart on pages 50–53). The design is stitched three times on 18 count snow blue Aida, each part then backed with iron-on interfacing before being mounted into the three sides of the pot according to the manufacturer's instructions.

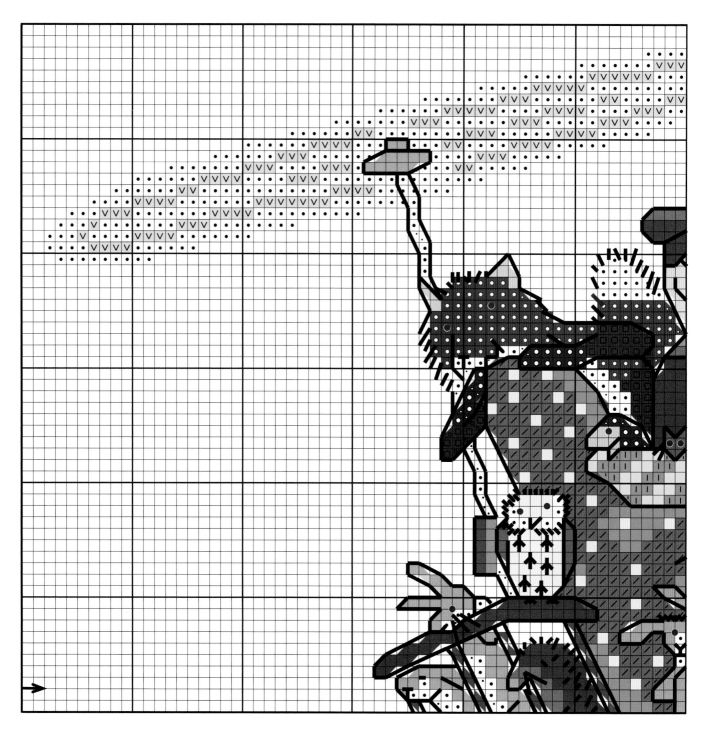

PERCY'S ART FOLDER KEY

DMC stranded cotton

Cross stitch

▨ 223	☑ 415	▨ 840	▨ 945	☐ 3779	
▨ 318	▨ 612	▨ 841	◎ 3023	▨ 3799	
▨ 320	▨ 726	▨ 900	− 3024	• B5200	
▨ 367	▨ 758	I 906	☐ 3047		
▨ 368	▨ 781	▨ 920	▨ 3722		

Backstitch/Long stitch

— 906

— 3799

French knots

● 3799

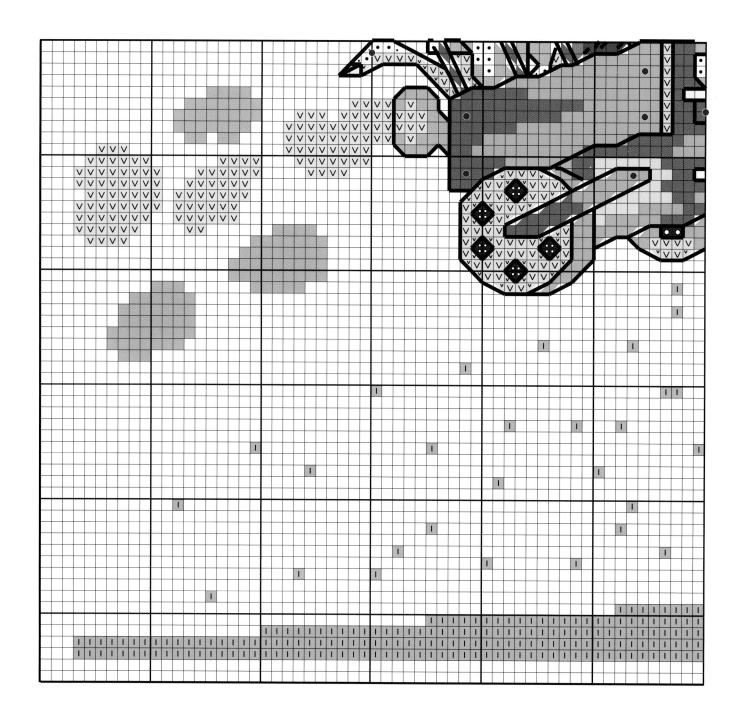

PERCY'S ART FOLDER KEY

DMC stranded cotton

Cross stitch

▨ 223	⋁ 415	▨ 840	▨ 945	▢ 3779	*Backstitch/Long stitch*	
▨ 318	▨ 612	▨ 841	⊙ 3023	◉ 3799	▬ 906	
▨ 320	▢ 726	◉ 900	— 3024	• B5200	▬ 3799	
▨ 367	▨ 758	I 906	▢ 3047		*French knots*	
▢ 368	▨ 781	▨ 920	╱ 3722		● 3799	

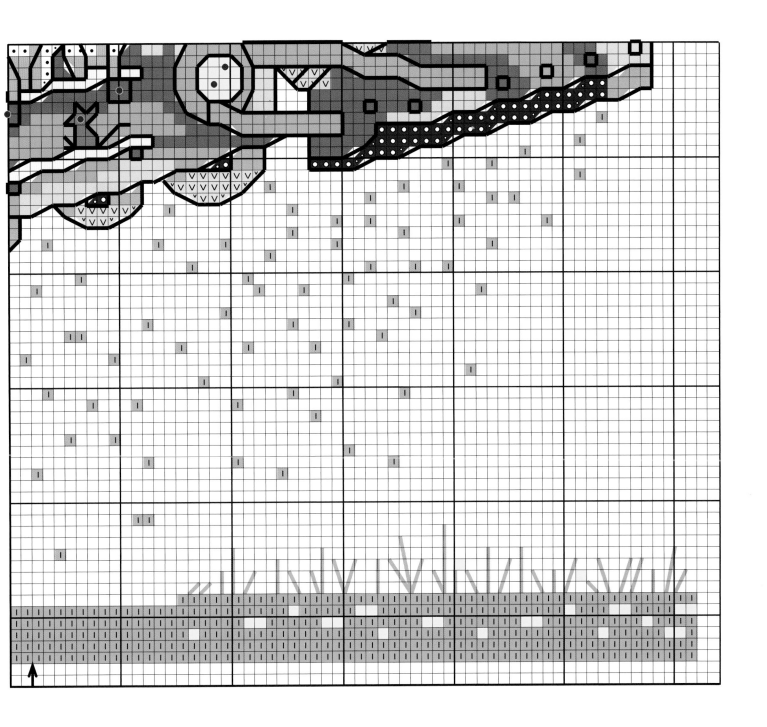

Birth Sampler

This charming sampler features Percy and his animal friends in their idyllic world – the characters are taken from many of Nick Butterworth's books. Percy is working hard in his park where there is always plenty to do. The fox, the hedgehog and the squirrels are in their new homes. Badger is up to mischief stealing from the picnic hamper and rabbit, who loves to play, is disturbed by mole who yet again has tunnelled up in an unexpected place.

STITCH COUNT
163 x 204

DESIGN SIZE
30 x 37cm (12 x 14½in) approx

WHAT YOU NEED

36 x 45cm (14 x 17⅛in) cream
14 count Aida

●

DMC stranded cotton (floss) as in
chart key

●

Tapestry needle

1 Prepare your fabric for work and mark the centre (see Techniques). Begin stitching from the centre following the charts on pages 50–53. Use two strands of stranded cotton (floss) for cross stitching and one for backstitching, outlining, long stitches and French knots.

2 Personalize the sampler by stitching the name and date of your choice within the dotted lines on the chart, using the alphabet and numbers charted on page 54. I used green (906) but you may prefer another colour. It is best to plan the name and date on graph paper before stitching (see page 105).

3 Once all the stitching is complete, press the embroidery carefully and then mount and frame.

STITCHING IDEAS

The individual designs could be stitched and framed to make a lovely collection of pictures. The separate designs could also be used on the front of a notebook or tote bag. Stitched over 14 count waste canvas (see Techniques, page 106) one of the designs could embellish a T-shirt.

ASHLEY
29th
AUGUST
2001

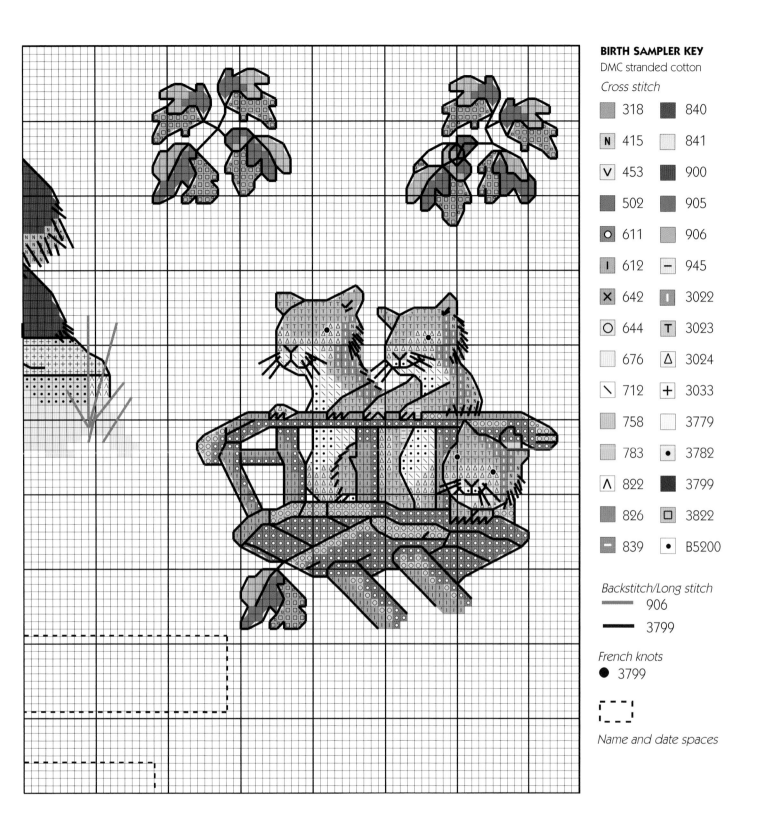

BIRTH SAMPLER KEY
DMC stranded cotton

Cross stitch

■	318	■	840
N	415	▢	841
V	453	■	900
■	502	■	905
O	611	■	906
I	612	−	945
×	642	I	3022
O	644	T	3023
▢	676	△	3024
\	712	+	3033
▨	758	▢	3779
▨	783	•	3782
∧	822	■	3799
■	826	▢	3822
−	839	•	B5200

Backstitch/Long stitch
——— 906
——— 3799

French knots
● 3799

┌ ─ ─ ┐
└ ─ ─ ┘

Name and date spaces

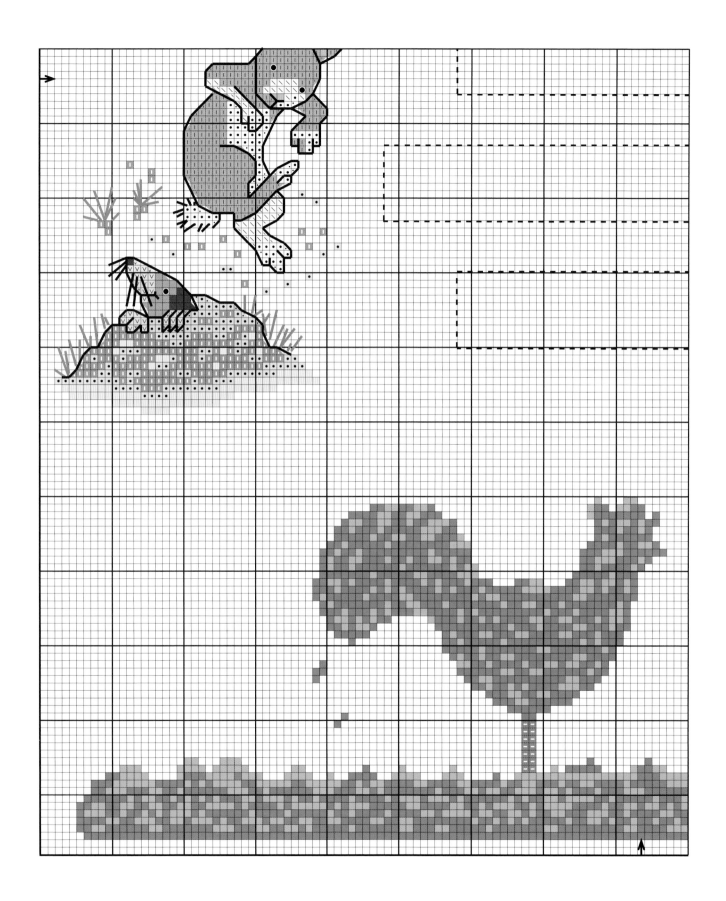

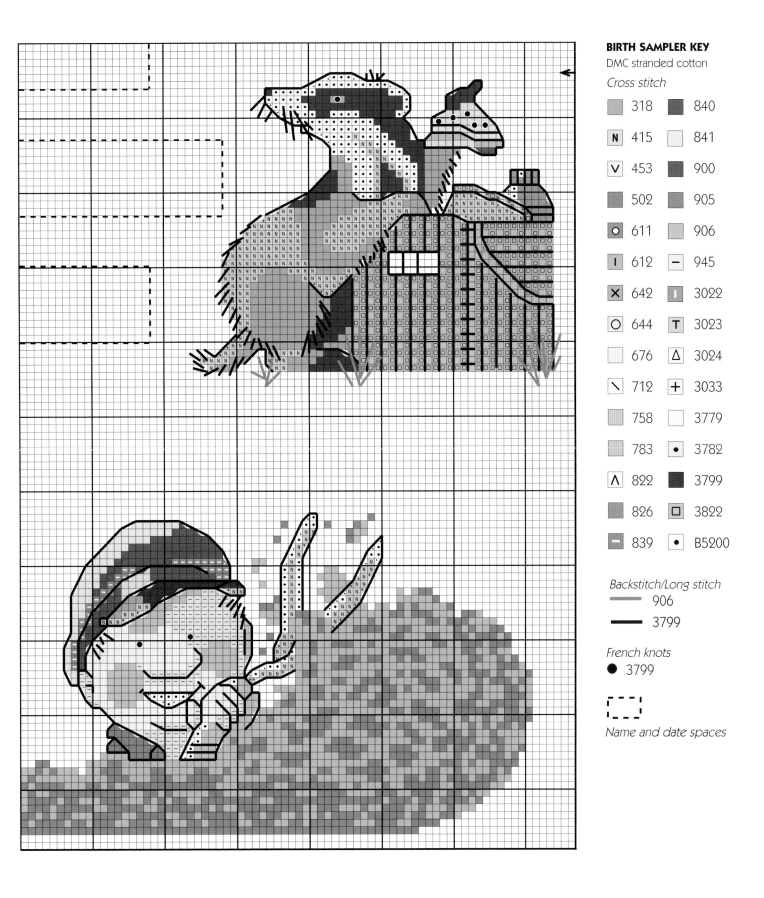

BIRTH SAMPLER KEY
DMC stranded cotton

Cross stitch

	318		840
N	415		841
V	453		900
	502		905
O	611		906
I	612	−	945
×	642	I	3022
O	644	T	3023
	676	Δ	3024
\	712	+	3033
	758		3779
	783	•	3782
Λ	822		3799
	826	□	3822
−	839	•	B5200

Backstitch/Long stitch

———— 906

———— 3799

French knots
● 3799

┌ ─ ┐
└ ─ ┘

Name and date spaces

BIRTH SAMPLER ALPHABET

Percy and his Animal Friends Picture

Percy the park keeper is having a well-earned rest from keeping his park tidy. The photograph overleaf shows him leaning over a wall admiring the view when all of a sudden he is joined by his animal friends. This design has been mounted in a rustic-looking frame and if hooks were screwed into the bottom it could be used for hanging a dressing gown or toy sack.

STITCH COUNT
170 x 81

DESIGN SIZE
31 x 15cm (12 x 5¾in) approx

WHAT YOU NEED

38 x 23cm (15 x 9in)
yellow 14 count Aida

●

DMC stranded cotton (floss) as in chart key

●

Tapestry needle

1 Prepare the fabric for work and mark the centre (see Techniques). Begin stitching from the centre following the chart on pages 58 and 59. Use two strands of stranded cotton (floss) for cross stitching and one strand for backstitching, outlining, long stitches and French knots.

2 When all the stitching has been completed, press the work carefully and then mount and frame.

PERCY AND HIS ANIMAL FRIENDS PICTURE KEY

DMC stranded cotton
Cross stitch

⊙ 318	562	Ⅰ 758	\ 945	N 3773	• B5200
– 320	611	775	946	3779	
367	612	← 780	950	◉ 3799	*Backstitch/Long stitch*
╱ 407	648	783	3032	M 3816	——— 3799
414	677	840	3064	3817	
z 415	746	841	▢ 3772	✕ 3820	*French knots* ● 3799

WALLACE AND GROMIT

Wallace and Gromit have captured the hearts of millions thanks to the imagination of Nick Park. The dynamic duo first appeared in *A Grand Day Out* – a wonderful adventure to the moon in a home-made rocket. They went on to become household names once *The Wrong Trousers* and *A Close Shave* were released by Aardman Animations.

The human half of the eccentric pair, Wallace, is a cheese-loving inventor: Gromit, his long-suffering dog, is the brains behind the duo. They are always plotting new adventures and get into many scrapes along the way. Wallace and Gromit have a huge fan base, which is no surprise as they have won over ninety international awards, including Academy Awards for *The Wrong Trousers* and *A Close Shave*, and a BAFTA and the Cartoon D'Or for *The Wrong Trousers*. These lovable characters are now contemporary classics known all over the world.

The projects in this chapter are great fun to stitch as they feature Wallace and Gromit in numerous escapades. The designs are perfect for creating all sorts of items, such as a novel porthole picture (shown here) and a duffle bag, and there are many ideas for making them up in other ways. Shaun, a quiet, modest sheep, features on a cushion cover. A delightfully cuddly animal with big, doleful eyes, he wanders in and out of trouble in *A Close Shave* without realizing he was ever there.

Porthole Picture

Wallace and Gromit don't do anything by half. Their idea of *A Grand Day Out* is to make a space rocket and fly off to check out the flavour of the cheesy moon. In this design they are shown looking out of a porthole window deciding on the best place to land for a picnic of moon cheese and crackers. The design has been framed using circular mount boards in black and white to look like a porthole. A circular wooden frame, which was spray painted pewter, completes the effect (see page 61).

STITCH COUNT
80 x 80

DESIGN SIZE
15cm (5¾in) diameter approx

WHAT YOU NEED

24 x 24cm (9½ x 9⅛in)
buttermilk 28 count Jobelan
(Fabric Flair NJ429.24)

DMC stranded cotton (floss)
as in chart key

Tapestry needle

Sheet of white mount board

Sheet of black mount board

Strong thread for lacing

Double-sided adhesive tape

1 Prepare your fabric for work and mark the centre (see Techniques). Begin stitching from the centre over two fabric threads following the chart. Use two strands of stranded cotton (floss) for cross stitching and one strand for backstitching, outlining and French knots for the eye highlights. When stitching is complete press the work carefully.

2 Cut a circle of white mount board 19cm (7½in) in diameter. Trim the embroidery to overlap this circle by at least 2.5cm (1in). Now stretch the embroidery on to the mount board circle, keeping the design taut by lacing it across the back with strong thread.

3 It is recommended that you get a professional framer to finish the picture. However if you do it yourself, start by preparing the white inner

mount ring by using a scalpel or craft knife to cut a 24cm (9½in) diameter circle out of white mount board. Now cut out the central portion, which should measure 13.5cm (5½in) in diameter, or to overlap the outer edge of the stitching. In the same way, cut out the outer ring from black mount board, with a 24cm (9½in) outer diameter and a 23cm (9in) inner diameter.

4 Fix the black ring centrally over the white ring using double-sided tape or spray glue to secure it in position. Place the rings over the embroidery, positioning the stitching centrally, and fix in place with double-sided tape.

5 To complete the picture, spray paint a 24cm (9½in) circular wooden frame with pewter paint. Then mount the picture within the frame, taping it down with masking tape on the back.

STITCHING IDEAS

This design would look wonderful stitched onto a T-shirt or sweatshirt using 14 count waste canvas. The design would also make a fun tablemat for a child, stitched centrally within a 23 x 28cm (9 x 11in) piece of white or cream 14 count Aida, with edges finished in contrasting bias binding.

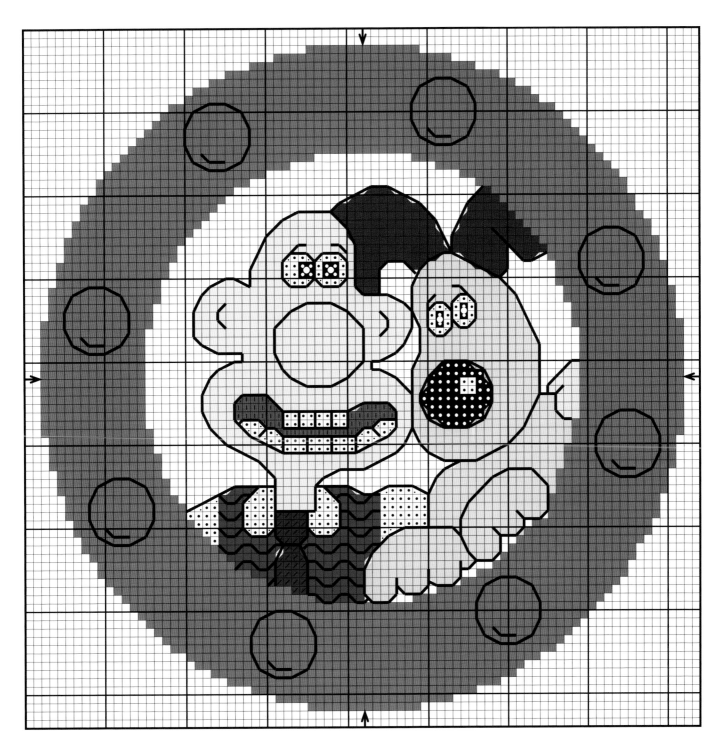

PORTHOLE PICTURE KEY

DMC stranded cotton

Cross stitch

☐ 225	◩ 666	☐ 738
◙ 310	▦ 699	▦ 3830
▦ 433	▓ 721	• B5200

Backstitch

— 310

French knots

○ B5200

Moonscape Duffel Bag

In *A Grand Day Out*, our two adventurous friends have landed on the moon and have settled down for a fine picnic of crackers and cheese. Wallace is keen to discover if the moon tastes any better than his beloved Wensleydale cheese. This wonderful scene has been used on a panel on the front of a really handy duffel bag.

STITCH COUNT
90 x 120

DESIGN SIZE
16.5 x 22cm (6½ x 8⅝in) approx

WHAT YOU NEED

20 x 28cm (8 x 11in) navy blue 14 count Aida

●

DMC stranded cotton (floss) as in chart key

●

DMC silver thread 5283

●

Tapestry needle

●

70 x 115cm (27½ x 45in) tangerine fleece

●

51cm (20in) contrasting ric-rac braid

●

Eight 11mm brass eyelets and tool

●

2m (2yd) navy cord

1 Prepare your fabric for work and mark the centre (see Techniques). Use an embroidery frame if you wish. Begin stitching from the centre following the chart on pages 68/69 using two strands of stranded cotton (floss) for cross stitching, backstitching and outlining except for the moon which is outlined with one strand of silver thread. The dotted lines on the chart denote the design's top edges. Once the stitching is complete, press the embroidery carefully on the reverse.

2 To make the duffel bag, start by cutting the tangerine fleece fabric as follows:
Two strips 7 x 23.5cm (2¾ x 9¼in) for the front panels;
One piece 41 x 65cm (16 x 25¾in) for the main body;
One piece 10 x 65cm (4 x 25¾in) for the bottom panel;
One circle 22cm (8¾in) diameter for the base;
One piece 5 x 13cm (2 x 5in) for the tab and slider.

3 For the two front panels either side of the embroidery panel, hand sew ric-rac braid down the centre of the two 7 x 23.5cm (2¾ x 9¼in) strips and then turn under 1cm (½in) along both long edges and tack (baste).

4 Trim the embroidery to 2.5cm (1in) from the edge of the stitching. Lay out the large main body piece of fleece and place the embroidery in the middle of this about 11.5cm (4½in) down from the top edge (see Fig 1 overleaf). Pin the tacked (basted) front strips down the outside edge of the embroidery, overlapping slightly with right sides up. Machine stitch down either side of these strips and then remove tacking (basting) threads.

5 Turn down 1cm (½in) along the top edge of the main body piece and tack (baste). Fold over again until the fleece is along the edge of the embroidery, overlapping slightly (see Fig 2 overleaf). Pin, tack (baste) and then machine stitch.

6 Take the 10 x 65cm (4 x 25¾in) bottom panel of fleece and turn under a 1cm (½in) hem on one long edge. In the same way as for the side panels, pin the fleece along the bottom edge of the embroidery and machine stitch close to the fold all the way along the main body piece. Remove pins and tacking (basting) thread.

7 Fold the whole bag panel in half with the embroidery facing out and machine stitch a 1cm (½in) seam down

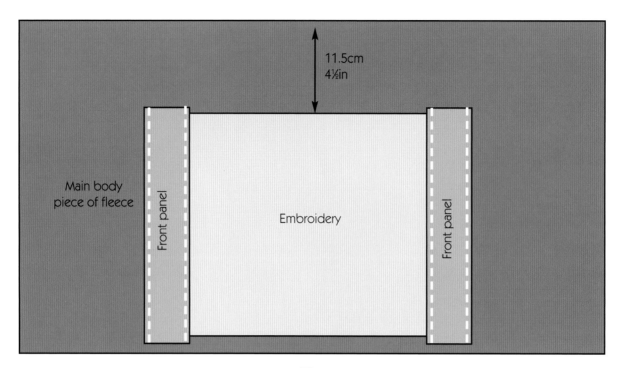

11.5cm
4½in

Main body
piece of fleece

Front panel

Embroidery

Front panel

Fig 1

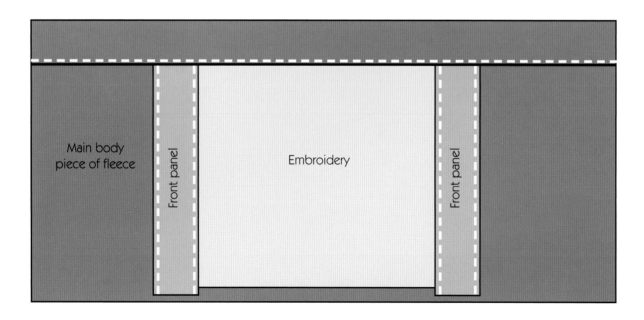

Main body
piece of fleece

Front panel

Embroidery

Front panel

Fig 2

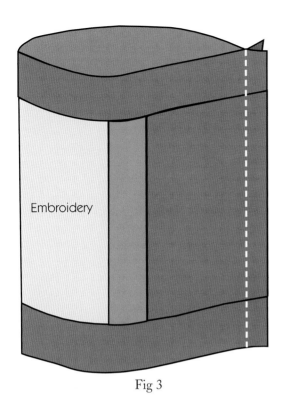

Fig 3

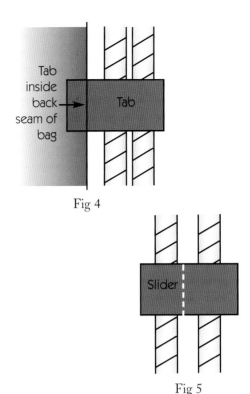

Fig 4

Fig 5

the short edge, then press open (see Fig 3). Turn the bag through so that the right sides are facing and re-stitch the seam 1cm (½in) from the edge to make a French seam, with the raw edges enclosed.

8 Now attach the base circle of fleece, with the bag inside out and right sides together, by carefully pinning and tacking (basting) the circle to the sides of the bag all round. Machine stitch 2cm (¾in) approximately from the edge all round. Turn the bag right way out.

9 Mark out eight eyelet holes equally around the top border of the bag, ensuring that there is one either side of the back seam. Use the insertion tool and follow the manufacturer's instructions for fitting the eyelets. Thread the navy cord through the eyelets, beginning and ending at the back seam.

10 To make a tab to hold the cord at the base of the bag, take a 13cm (5in) long strip of fleece 5cm (2in) wide, fold in half lengthways and machine stitch a seam. Cut a 6cm (2½in) long piece from this strip and fold in half. At the base of the bag snip some of the seam stitches, tuck the raw edges of the tab inside the seam and re-stitch the seam (see Fig 4).

11 To make a slider for the cord, fold the remaining piece of the strip around the cord and machine stitch between the cords to secure (see Fig 5). Slip the ends of the cord into the tab and tie in a knot to finish.

STITCHING IDEAS

This design would look great on the front of a ready-made bag. Once the stitching is complete, make a seam around all four sides and slipstitch on to the front of the bag. Finish the edges using contrasting ric-rac braid. The design is such a fun one it would also be delightful framed – for children and adults alike to enjoy.

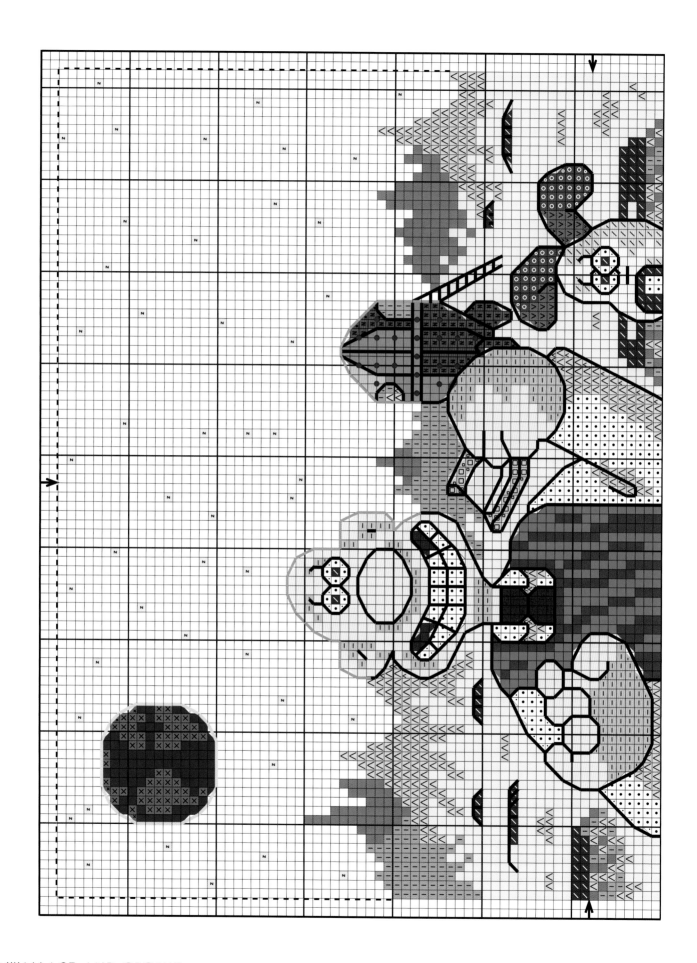

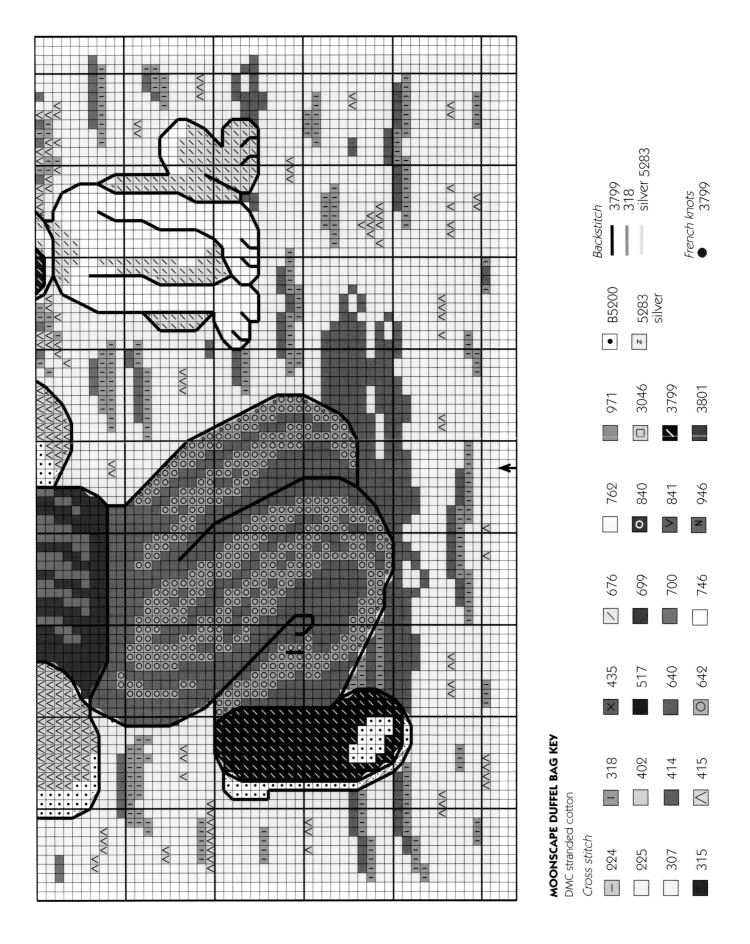

MOONSCAPE DUFFEL BAG KEY

DMC stranded cotton

Cross stitch

	224		318		971	•	B5200
	225		402		3046	z	5283 silver
	307		414		3799	
	315		415		3801	
	676		762			
	699		840			
	700		841			
	746		946			
X	435					
	517					
	640					
O	642					

Backstitch

3799
318
silver 5283

French knots
● 3799

Shaun's Cushion

Shaun the sheep is famous for wandering in and out of scrapes without ever seeming to know he is there – as long as there is something to eat, he's happy. This lovable character from *A Close Shave* has been stitched on to a lovely pale blue evenweave fabric and placed in the middle of a cuddly cushion.

STITCH COUNT
90 x 100

DESIGN SIZE
16.5 x 18cm (6½ x 7in)
approx

WHAT YOU NEED

25 x 24cm (10 x 9½in)
light blue 28 count
Jobelan (NJ429.21)

●

Danish Flower thread as
in chart key

●

Rainbow Gallery Whisper
thread as in chart key

●

DMC stranded cotton
(floss) as in chart key

●

Tapestry needle

●

50cm (20in) purple
gingham fabric

●

18 x 18cm (7 x 7in) pink
gingham fabric

●

2m (2yd) purple
ric-rac braid

●

3m (118in) bobble braid

●

Matching sewing thread

●

36 x 36cm (14 x 14in)
cushion pad

1 Prepare your fabric and mark the centre (see Techniques). Begin stitching from the centre over two fabric threads following the chart overleaf. Use two strands of stranded cotton (floss) for cross stitching and one strand for Danish Flower thread and all backstitching and outlining. Use Rainbow Gallery Whisper thread for the French knots. Once stitching is complete press the work.

2 To make the cushion, first trim the Jobelan fabric to 21cm (8½in) square. Now cut out the gingham fabrics as follows:
One purple square
38 x 38cm (15 x 15in) for the back;
Four purple rectangles
9 x 20cm (3½x 8in) for the front panels;
Four pink squares
9 x 9cm (3½ x 3½in) for the front panels.

3 With right sides facing and with 1cm (½in) seam allowances, sew the cut pieces into three strips as follows (see diagram on page 73). Machine stitch a pink gingham square to each of the short ends of two of the purple gingham rectangles. Now stitch the other two purple gingham rectangles to the top and bottom of the embroidered square.

4 Press the seams open, then pin and stitch one narrow strip to either side of the wide central strip. Press the two long seams open. Hand stitch ric-rac braid over the joined edges of the gingham pieces (see photograph). This not only looks attractive but will cover any inaccuracies in the joins.

5 Fold the length of bobble braid in half and pin it around the edges of the cushion front, with raw edges matching, and tack (baste) in position. Place the purple gingham square for the cushion back onto the cushion front with right sides facing. Stitch the edges of the cushion close to the edge of the bobble braid leaving a gap to insert a cushion pad.

6 Snip the corners, then turn the cushion cover right side out and press. Insert a cushion pad and slipstitch the opening. Alternatively, sew a length of Velcro to the two open edges of the cushion cover, insert the cushion and close the Velcro fastening.

SHAUN'S CUSHION KEY

Cross stitch

- DMC stranded cotton B5200

  Danish flower thread 31

  Danish flower thread 2

  Danish flower thread 230

  Danish flower thread 240

Backstitch/Long stitch
— DMC stranded cotton 3799

French knots
○   Rainbow Gallery Whisper thread W88

Pink square		Purple rectangle		Pink square
		Embroidery		
Purple rectangle				Purple rectangle
Pink square		Purple rectangle		Pink square

STITCHING IDEAS

Stitch Shaun into a patch pocket and use to decorate the front of an apron, a bib or a pair of dungarees. Alternatively Shaun would look great on the front of a pattern holder and I am sure that if he were stitched on a smaller count fabric, such as an 18 or 22, and made into a card he would delight the receiver on any special occasion.

Why not change the design slightly as shown below, and stitch a row of brightly coloured wall balls on an Aida or linen band? This would be very appropriate sewn on to a knitting bag.

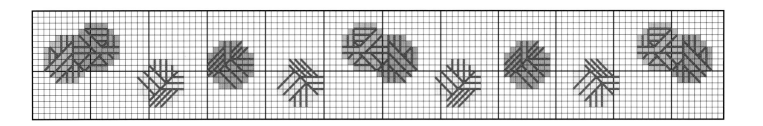

HARRY AND THE BUCKETFUL OF DINOSAURS

When Harry helps his Nan to clear out the attic he finds a dusty old box and lifting the lid he makes a wonderful discovery – DINOSAURS! He washes them, unbends them, fixes the broken ones and puts them in a bucket. He learns all their names and takes them everywhere with him – out shopping, to the garden centre, to the beach, even in the bath. But one sad day Harry loses his bucketful of dinosaurs on a train and has to prove to the Lost Property Man that they really belong to him. This charming story, written by Ian Whybrow and beautifully illustrated by Adrian Reynolds, demonstrates the power of the imagination of young children.

In this chapter you will find Harry's dinosaurs on the pockets of a toy tidy (shown here), where young children can hide their precious keepsakes. A toy sack, featuring Harry with his bucket filled with dinosaurs is another useful place for keeping toys tidy. These projects are great fun, as everyone loves dinosaurs, and there are many suggestions for other ways the designs could be used.

Illustrations © Adrian Reynolds 2000

Dinosaurs Toy Tidy

Harry, like most of us, is fascinated by dinosaurs and he goes to the library to find out all their names – anchisaurus, apatosaurus, scelidosaurus, stegosaurus, triceratops and tyrannosaurus. Here, his dinosaurs have been transformed into six wonderfully versatile designs.

WHAT YOU NEED

Six pieces 25.5 x 22cm (10 x 8½in) yellow 14 count Aida

DMC stranded cotton (floss) as in chart key

Tapestry needle

75cm (30in) green ric-rac braid

65 x 56cm (25½ x 22in) dark green cotton fabric

65 x 56cm (25½ x 22in) backing fabric

Matching sewing threads

Six 15cm (6in) lengths of ribbon

Length of wooden doweling for hanging

1 Start by making the pockets using the Aida pieces. For each pocket press a 4cm (1½in) turning to the right side along the long top edge, then machine stitch along 2.5cm (1in) from the top using matching sewing thread. Fray the edge by teasing out the threads. Stitch lengths of green ric-rac braid 1cm (½in) from the top along the top edges of all the pockets. Press 1.5cm (⅝in) seams to the wrong side along the other three edges.

2 Mark the centre of each pocket and begin cross stitching each dinosaur design from here, following the charts. Use two strands of stranded cotton (floss) for cross stitching and one strand for backstitching, outlining and French knots. Please note that the stitch counts and design sizes for each dinosaur appear with the charts.

3 Arrange the pockets in two columns on the right side of the dark green fabric, 7cm (2¾in) from the top edge, and 2.5cm (1in) from the side and bottom edges (see picture). Pin, tack (baste) and then stitch the pockets in place along their side and bottom edges. Remove pins and tacking.

4 Fold the lengths of ribbon in half so the short edges meet and form a loop. Pin the ribbons to the top edge of the green fabric with right sides facing and raw edges matching (making a 'sandwich'). Now pin, tack (baste) and stitch the green fabric and backing fabric together, leaving a gap along a side edge for turning. Snip the seams at the corners, turn right sides out and close the gap by oversewing before pressing. To finish, thread the wooden doweling through the loops and hang.

STITCHING IDEAS

Stitch the designs on to 18 count fabric and make single patches for clothing or a bag front. Each of the dinosaurs could also feature in cards. If you stitched all the dinosaurs on to a single piece of fabric they would make a lovely sampler to hang in a child's bedroom. If you have a personal favourite, stitch the design and mount it in a free-standing frame for a desk.

TYRANNOSAURUS

(tie-RAN-oh-SAW-rus)

STEGOSAURUS

(STEG-oh-SAW-rus)

TRICERATOPS

(try-SER-a-tops)

ANCHISAURUS

(AN-ki-SAW-rus)

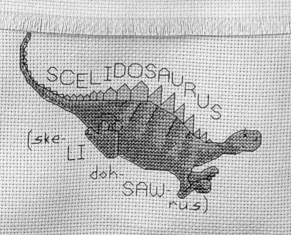

SCELIDOSAURUS

(ske-LI-doh-SAW-rus)

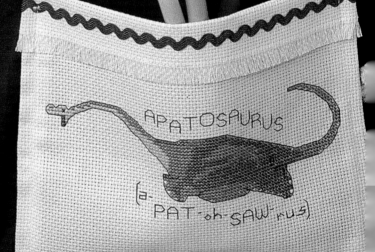

APATOSAURUS

(a-PAT-oh-SAW-rus)

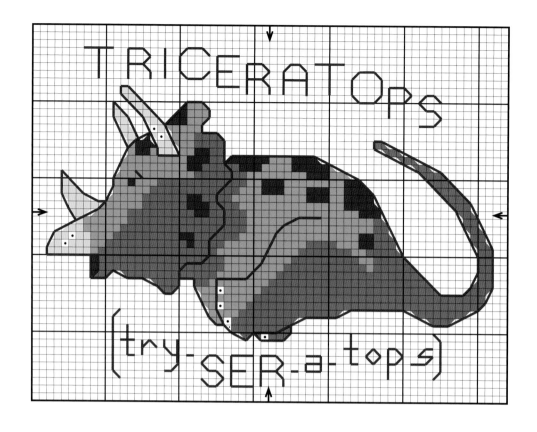

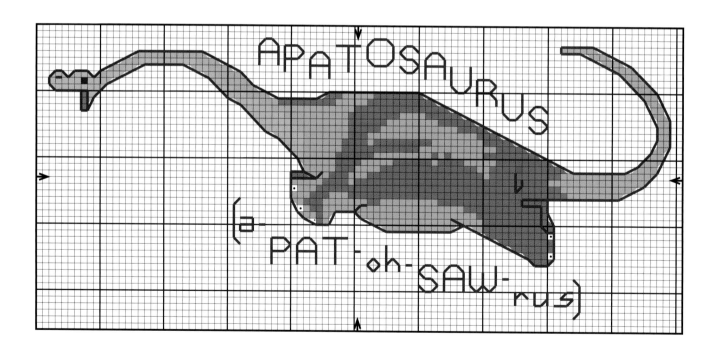

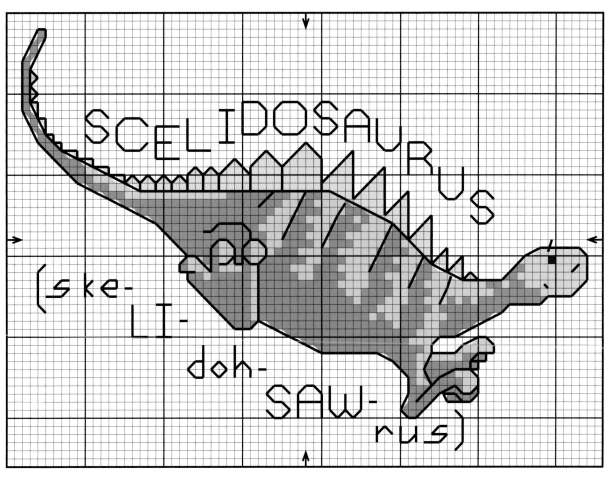

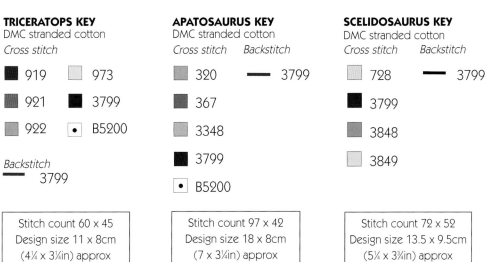

TRICERATOPS KEY
DMC stranded cotton
Cross stitch

■	919	▨	973
▨	921	■	3799
▨	922	•	B5200

Backstitch
— 3799

Stitch count 60 x 45
Design size 11 x 8cm
(4¼ x 3¼in) approx

APATOSAURUS KEY
DMC stranded cotton
Cross stitch   *Backstitch*

▨	320	—	3799
▨	367		
▨	3348		
■	3799		
•	B5200		

Stitch count 97 x 42
Design size 18 x 8cm
(7 x 3¼in) approx

SCELIDOSAURUS KEY
DMC stranded cotton
Cross stitch   *Backstitch*

▨	728	—	3799
■	3799		
▨	3848		
▨	3849		

Stitch count 72 x 52
Design size 13.5 x 9.5cm
(5¼ x 3¾in) approx

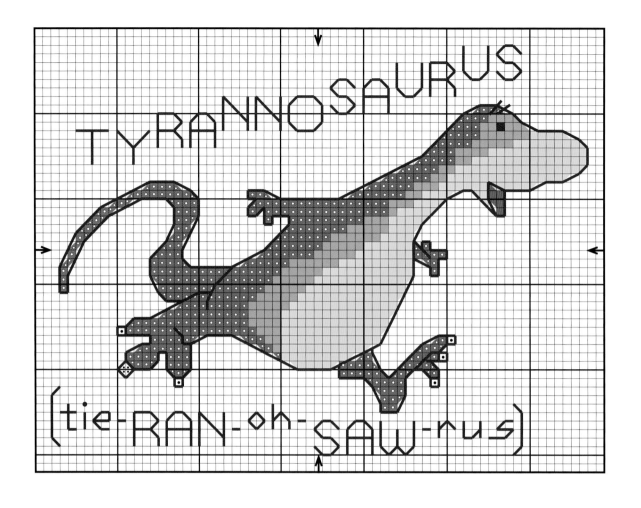

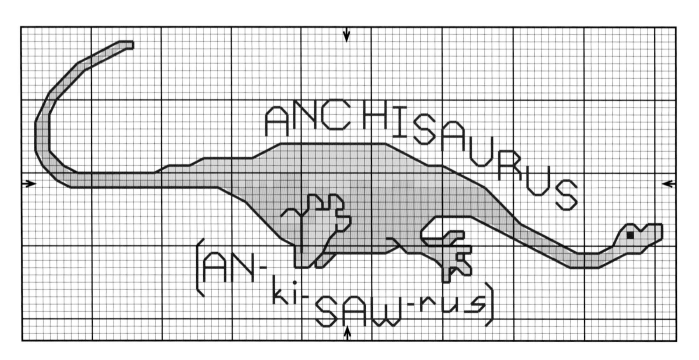

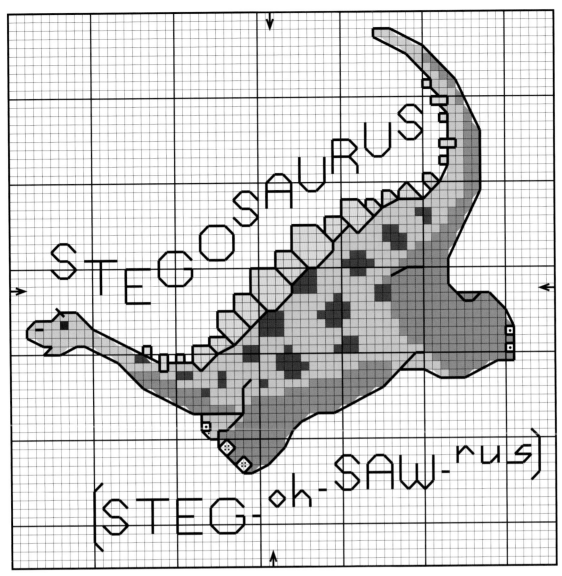

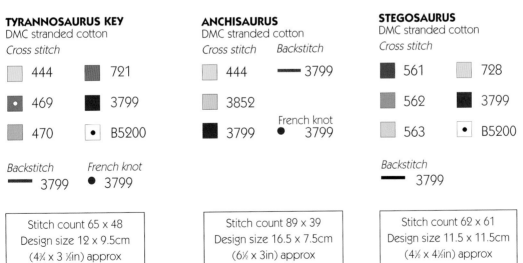

TYRANNOSAURUS KEY
DMC stranded cotton

Cross stitch

▢	444	▨	721
▣	469	■	3799
▨	470	⊡	B5200

Backstitch   *French knot*
— 3799   ● 3799

Stitch count 65 x 48
Design size 12 x 9.5cm
(4¾ x 3 ⅛in) approx

ANCHISAURUS
DMC stranded cotton

Cross stitch   *Backstitch*

▢	444	—	3799
▨	3852		
■	3799		

French knot
● 3799

Stitch count 89 x 39
Design size 16.5 x 7.5cm
(6½ x 3in) approx

STEGOSAURUS
DMC stranded cotton

Cross stitch

■	561	▨	728
▨	562	■	3799
▢	563	⊡	B5200

Backstitch
— 3799

Stitch count 62 x 61
Design size 11.5 x 11.5cm
(4½ x 4½in) approx

Harry's Toy Sack

Harry loves his dinosaurs and knows all their names – which turns out to be very useful in the end. He takes them everywhere in a bucket because they hate boxes. This lovely image of Harry with the dinosaurs has been made into a bright and cheerful toy sack.

STITCH COUNT

111 x 127

DESIGN SIZE

20 x 23cm (8 x 9in) approx

WHAT YOU NEED

50cm x 1.12m (20 x 44in) light blue 28 count Jobelan (Fabric Flair NJ429.21)

●

DMC stranded cotton (floss) as in chart key

●

Tapestry needle

●

Two pieces 7 x 47cm (2¾ x 18½in) contrasting fabric

●

Matching sewing thread

●

White twisted cord

1 Fold the embroidery fabric in half so that the short ends meet and the fold is the bottom. Begin stitching 10cm (4in) up from the fold following the chart overleaf. Use two strands of stranded cotton (floss) for cross stitching and one strand for backstitching, outlining and French knots.

2 To make up the sack, take the two pieces of contrasting fabric (channels for the cord) and press a 1cm (½in) turning all round each strip. With right sides up, centre a channel strip over the unfolded embroidered fabric, 7cm (2¾in) from each short edge. Tack (baste) the strips in place, then stitch along each long edge of each strip, leaving the short edges open to form the drawstring channel.

3 Fold the embroidered fabric in half with right sides together so that the short edges meet. Pin and stitch the two long seams, taking a 1.5cm (⅝in) seam allowance. Then stitch a 1.5cm (⅝in) hem along the top edge. Trim the excess seam allowance at the corners to reduce bulk and turn the bag right side out. To finish, thread the white cord through the channel and knot the ends.

STITCHING IDEAS

This design would look charming mounted in a frame for a child's bedroom. It could also be used on the front of a book cover or photograph album.

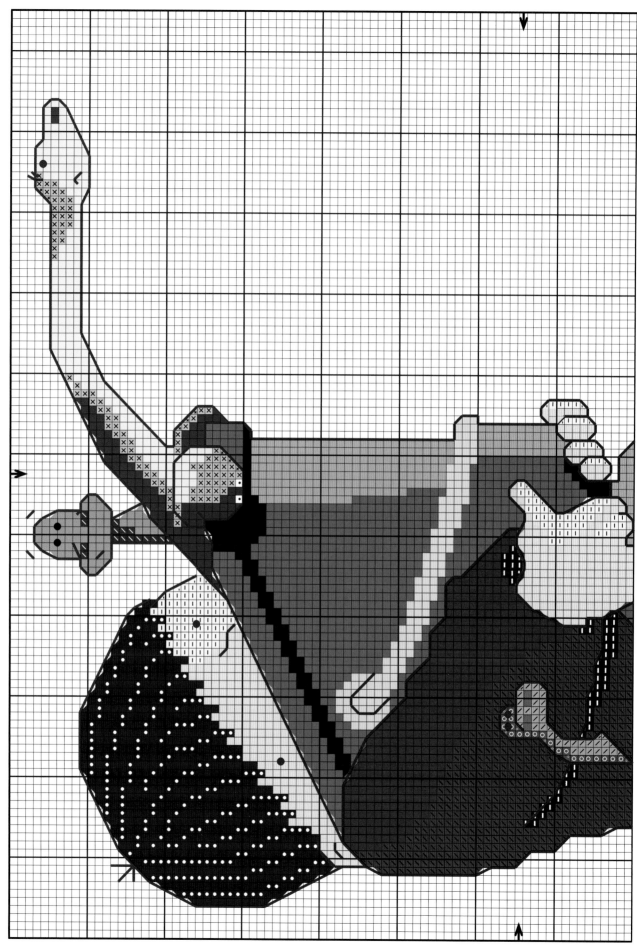

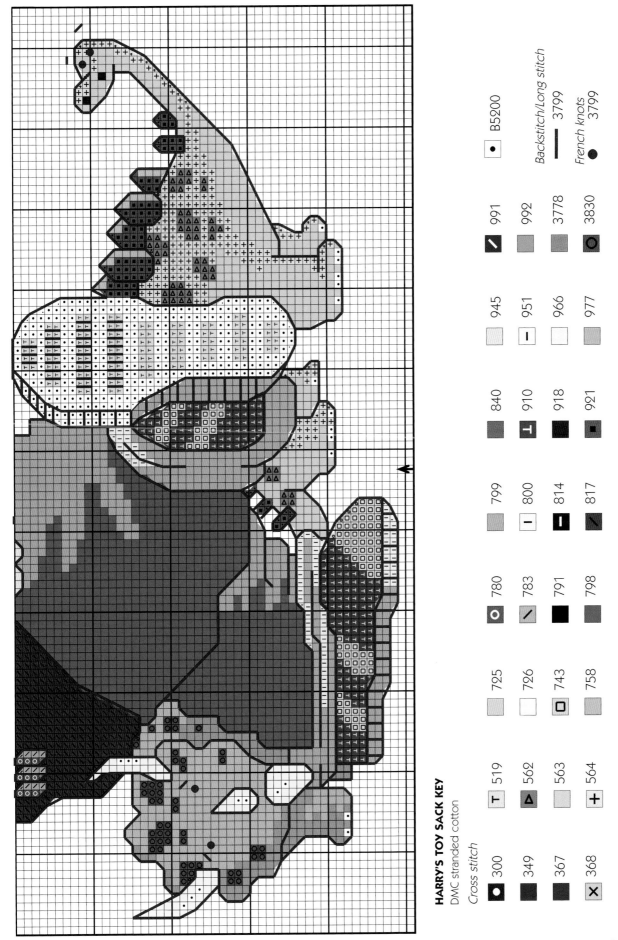

HARRY'S TOY SACK KEY

DMC stranded cotton

Cross stitch

◨	300	◨	519	
◼	349	▲	562	
◼	367	◼	563	
✕	368	✚	564	

◉	780	◼	725	◼	799
◢	783	◻	726	▬	800
◼	791	◻	743	◼	814
◼	798	◼	758	◥	817

◼	840	◼	945	◼	991
◨	910	◻	951	◼	992
◼	918	◻	966	◼	3778
◼	921	◼	977	◉	3830

◉	B5200

Backstitch/Long stitch

—	3799

French knots

●	3799

MR MEN AND LITTLE MISS

It is hard to believe that Roger Hargreaves created the dynamic characters of Mr Men and Little Miss over thirty years ago. He believed in keeping things simple and by using strong colours and a simple style he produced instantly recognisable characters with human personalities. Today there are forty-three Mr Men and thirty Little Miss characters in total.

The characters are fun for the young at heart, be they children or adults, because they are full of adventure and sometimes pure nonsense, which amuses and entertains us. Each character has individual appeal and each one is part of us. Everyone can point to a smiling Mr Happy, a clumsy Mr Bump and a playful Little Miss Giggles in real life. The whole family is sure to be delighted with these bright, cheerful designs with their cheeky sense of fun and mischief.

The designs are extremely versatile and can be used for a multitude of purposes, as shown by the many projects in this chapter. Mr Men and Little Miss can be used in various cards to celebrate a special occasion such as a birthday or they can be sewn on a large square of Afghan fabric to brighten up a child's bedroom. They look terrific when sewn as a patch or pocket on clothing or accessories and they can be used in many other ways, including a make-up bag, a mobile phone holder and a boot bag.

Little Miss Throw

Little Miss are full of fun and make ideal subjects for a bright and cheerful pram cover using Afghan fabric, a soft evenweave with tramlines running through it to create squares (see photograph on previous page). Along with a bold flower motif, this project features Little Miss Sunshine, Little Miss Scatterbrain, Little Miss Naughty, Little Miss Fun and Little Miss Bossy.

WHAT YOU NEED

74 x 74cm (29 x 29in) white 18 count Afghan (Anne) evenweave fabric (Zweigart E753)

●

DMC stranded cotton (floss) as in chart key

●

Tapestry needle

●

Matching sewing thread

1 Prepare your fabric for work, and mark the centre of each square. Please note that stitch counts and design sizes for each Little Miss appear with the charts and have been calculated over two threads of 18 count evenweave (i.e. divide the stitch counts by 9). Begin stitching each design from the centre of the individual squares over two threads of the Afghan fabric following the charts. Use two strands of cotton (floss) for the cross stitching and backstitching.

2 To finish the Afghan, trim the stitched fabric around the outer tramline edge allowing 7.5cm (3in) for a fringe. Using matching sewing thread, run several rows of machine stitching around the edge of the outer tramlines to prevent fraying. Now tease out the threads at the outer edges to make a fringe.

STITCHING IDEAS

You could mix Mr Men and Little Miss to make a larger Afghan as a throw over a chair or bed, or why not stitch a smaller piece to make into a cushion cover?

Baby Brick

A baby brick is an excellent way to use the Mr Men and Little Miss designs. You could choose a selection of Mr Men and Little Miss or, as here, Little Miss alone. Using the same Afghan fabric as in the pram blanket, the designs have been stitched over one thread this time and edged with a cheery border. This demonstrates the difference in sizes between stitching over one or two strands of a fabric.

WHAT YOU NEED

Six 15cm (6in) squares of white 18 count Afghan (Anne) evenweave fabric (Zweigart E753)

●

DMC stranded cotton as in chart key

●

Tapestry needle

●

Six 15cm (6in) squares of medium-weight iron-on interfacing

●

Polyester wadding (batting)

●

Matching sewing thread

1 Prepare your fabric for work and mark the centres of the six Afghan squares. Begin stitching from the centre of each square over one fabric thread following the charts. Use two strands of stranded cotton (floss) for cross stitch. Complete six squares, adding a border of several rows of mixed, brightly coloured cross stitch (see chart on page 91).

2 Carefully iron the squares of interfacing on to the back of each of the designs to give added strength to the fabric and keep the stitches secure.

3 To make up the brick, use one square as a base, then with right sides facing, pin and tack (baste) an embroidered square on to each of the four edges of the base square. Stitch along the seams, close to the cross stitch border. Press the seams open. Now fold each square upwards so that the sides meet and, with right sides facing, stitch the matching sides together.

4 To finish, pin, tack (baste) and stitch the remaining square in place, stitching along three edges and leaving one edge open. Remove all pins and turn right side out. Fill with wadding (batting), then slipstitch the gap to close.

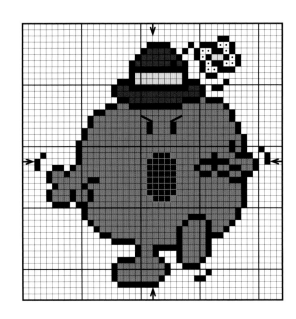

LITTLE MISS BOSSY KEY
DMC stranded cotton

Cross stitch		Backstitch	
■	310	▬	310
▨	825		
▨	725		
▨	666		
•	B5200		

Stitch count 40 x 40
Design size 11.25 x 11.25cm
(4⅛ x 4⅛in) approx

LITTLE MISS NAUGHTY KEY
DMC stranded cotton

Cross stitch

310	■
3746	▨
3850	▨

Stitch count 29 x 42
Design size 8 x 12cm
(3¼ x 5in) approx

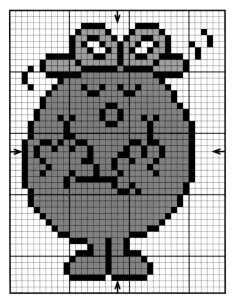

LITTLE MISS FUN KEY
DMC stranded cotton

Cross stitch		Backstitch	
■	310	▬	310
▨	976		
▨	3843		

Stitch count 42 x 40
Design size 12 x 11.25cm
(5 x 4⅛in) approx

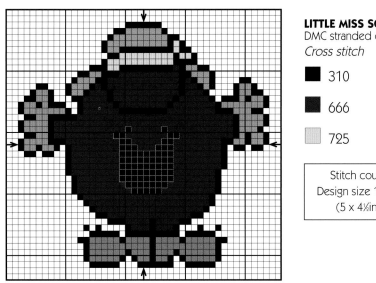

LITTLE MISS SCATTERBRAIN
DMC stranded cotton
Cross stitch

■	310	▨	3746
■	666	▨	3843
▢	725	▨	3850

Stitch count 42 x 40
Design size 12 x 11.25cm
(5 x 4⅛in) approx

**FLOWER
AND BORDER KEY**
DMC stranded cotton
Cross stitch

310	■
726	▢
3746	▨
3850	▨

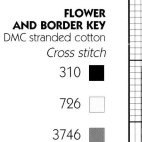

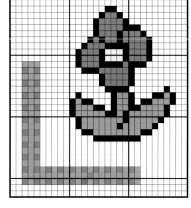

LITTLE MISS SUNSHINE KEY
DMC stranded cotton
Cross stitch

■	310
■	666
▨	725

Stitch count 42 x 36
Design size 12 x 10cm
(5 x 4in) approx

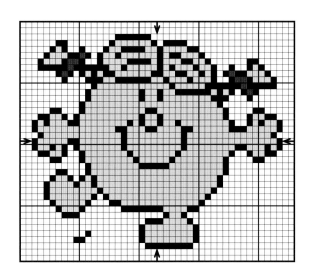

Mr Men Card Collection

It is always a pleasure to receive a hand-stitched card and as Mr Men are such fun they make ideal subjects. Mr Grumpy would definitely amuse a keen golfer and Mr Muddle is a winner for an angler. No birthday would be complete without a cake and Mr Greedy makes the ideal delivery boy. A smiling Mr Happy is perfect for offering congratulations on passing an examination or to cheer anyone up. Three more Mr Men charts can be found on page 104.

WHAT YOU NEED FOR EACH CARD

12.5 x 12.5cm (5 x 5in) white 28 count Jobelan

DMC stranded cotton (floss) as in chart keys

Tapestry needle

Double-sided adhesive tape

A card to fit and complement the design (see Suppliers)

1 Prepare your fabric for work and mark the centre (see Techniques). Please note that the stitch counts and design sizes for each Mr Men appear with the charts and have been calculated over two threads of a 28 count evenweave (i.e. divide the stitch counts by 14). Begin stitching from the centre over two fabric threads following the relevant chart. Use two strands of stranded cotton (floss) for cross stitching and one strand for backstitching.

2 When stitching is complete, place the card aperture centrally over the embroidery and trim the embroidery if necessary. Place double-sided tape on the back of the card aperture. Peel the backing off and position the card, right way up, over the embroidery. When you're happy with the position, press down firmly.

3 Turn the card over and place double-sided adhesive tape on the left-hand flap. Peel off the backing and fold the flap down to cover the back of the embroidery. For a padded look, you could stick wadding (batting) to the back of the embroidery using tape and then stick the flap down as before.

STITCHING IDEAS

These designs are extremely versatile and can be used in many other ways, for example, as patches on clothing, such as ready-made fleece jackets or T-shirts. Simply stitch the design on a 28 count evenweave fabric, then turn under a hem and slipstitch the patch to the garment. Similarly, a fleece hat, made from a purchased pattern, is a great place for showing off any of the designs. A scarf made from a long 25cm (10in) wide strip of fleece is also perfect for embellishing with Mr Men. For a finishing touch, cut and knot the ends of the scarf as in the bath pillow on page 16. The Mr Men designs can also be stitched on a smaller count fabric, such as an 18 count Aida or 32 count evenweave, which would enable them to be made into small items such as luggage labels and egg cosies. (See additional Mr Men charts on page 104.)

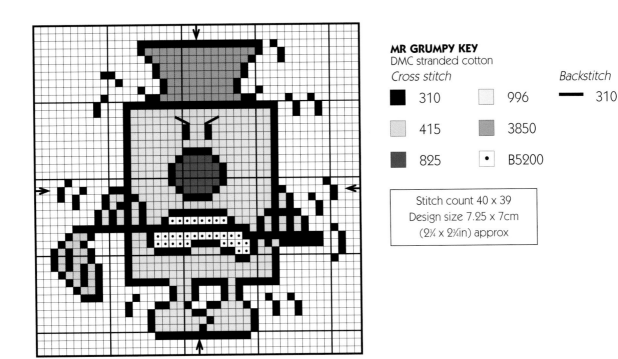

MR GRUMPY KEY
DMC stranded cotton
Cross stitch

					Backstitch
■	310	▫	996	▬	310
▨	415	▨	3850		
▨	825	⊡	B5200		

Stitch count 40 x 39
Design size 7.25 x 7cm
(2¾ x 2¾in) approx

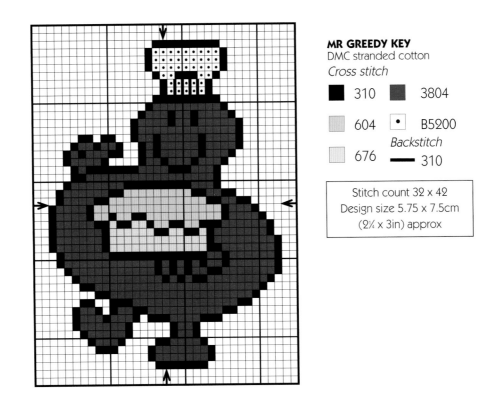

MR GREEDY KEY
DMC stranded cotton
Cross stitch

■	310	▨	3804
▨	604	⊡	B5200
			Backstitch
▨	676	▬	310

Stitch count 32 x 42
Design size 5.75 x 7.5cm
(2¼ x 3in) approx

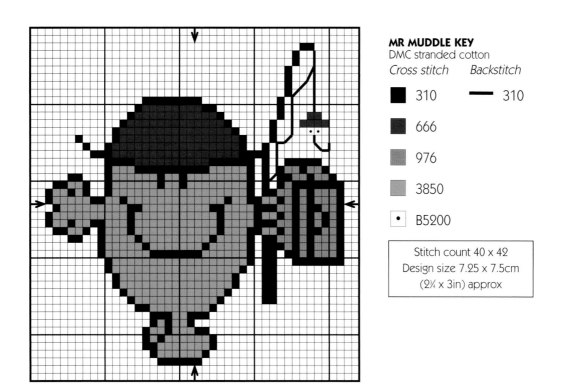

MR MUDDLE KEY
DMC stranded cotton

Cross stitch		Backstitch	
■	310	—	310
■	666		
■	976		
■	3850		
•	B5200		

Stitch count 40 x 42
Design size 7.25 x 7.5cm
(2¾ x 3in) approx

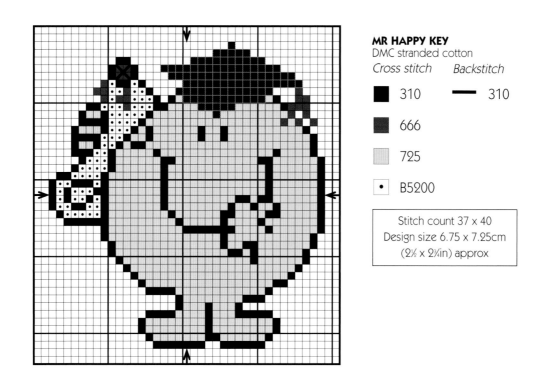

MR HAPPY KEY
DMC stranded cotton

Cross stitch		Backstitch	
■	310	—	310
■	666		
▦	725		
•	B5200		

Stitch count 37 x 40
Design size 6.75 x 7.25cm
(2⅝ x 2¾in) approx

Little Miss Splendid Tote Pocket

Little Miss Splendid has just paid a visit to the *Extra Expensive Shop*. . . every girl's favourite pastime, and now with all those purchases she needs an extra shopping bag for her personal items. She is featured here as a pocket on a ready-made tote bag, along with a Little Miss Chatterbox phone holder and a Little Miss Tiny make-up bag, both described overleaf.

STITCH COUNT
31 x 42

DESIGN SIZE
5.5 x 7.5cm (2¼ x 3in) approx

WHAT YOU NEED

25 x 20cm (10 x 8in) cream 28 count Meran fabric (DMC-E3972)

●

DMC stranded cotton (floss) as in chart key

●

Tapestry needle

●

25cm (10in) length beaded braid

●

Matching sewing thread

●

Ready-made tote bag

1 Prepare your fabric for work (see Techniques). Begin stitching 3.5cm (1½in) from the bottom of the fabric, stitching over two fabric threads following the chart on page 102. Use two strands of stranded cotton (floss) for cross stitch and one for backstitch.

2 To make the pocket, stitch a 1cm (½in) hem along the top edge of the fabric. Using matching sewing thread, sew the beaded braid on the right side of the fabric along this top edge.

3 Turn a 1cm (½in) hem around the sides and base and then hand sew the pocket on to the front of a ready-made tote bag.

STITCHING IDEAS

This design could be interchanged with one of the designs on the Afghan pram blanket or the baby brick. It would look great in the lid of a ceramic bowl or made into a card, especially for a shopaholic friend.

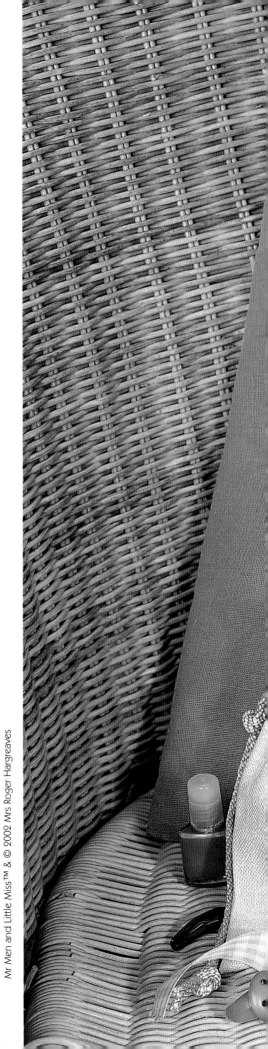

Mr Men and Little Miss™ & © 2002 Mrs Roger Hargreaves

Little Miss Chatterbox Phone Holder

Little Miss Chatterbox is a fun-loving girl who likes to chat with her friends — all the time! Mobile phones are increasingly popular with adults and children alike and Little Miss Chatterbox is the perfect choice for the front of a phone holder.

STITCH COUNT
40 x 42

DESIGN SIZE
7.5 x 7.5cm (3 x 3in) approx

WHAT YOU NEED

11.5 x 38cm (4½ x 15in) cream 28 count Meran fabric (DMC-E3270)

●

DMC stranded cotton (floss) as in key chart

●

Tapestry needle

●

11.5 x 38cm (4½ x 15in) lining fabric

●

Matching sewing thread

1 Prepare your fabric for work (see Techniques). Begin stitching 2.5cm (1in) up from the bottom of the fabric, stitching over two threads of the fabric following the chart on page 102. Use two strands of stranded cotton (floss) for the cross stitch and French knots (use either black or white for the French knots).

2 To make the mobile phone holder, place the embroidered fabric and the lining fabric right sides together and trim the bottom into a gentle curve (see photograph). Now pin, tack (baste) and stitch around three sides, leaving the short, straight edge open to allow for turning. Trim the seam, remove any pins and tacking (basting) and turn through to the right side.

3 Turn under a hem along the open edge and slipstitch to close. Fold over the top part of the holder. If you wish to fasten the holder you could either use a button and loop or a small piece of Velcro.

Little Miss Tiny Make-up Bag

Little Miss Tiny smiles endearingly from the front of a make up bag – an essential item for emergency repairs when out shopping with Little Miss Splendid.

STITCH COUNT
42 x 30

DESIGN SIZE
7.5 x 5.5cm (3in x 2¼in) approx

WHAT YOU NEED

20 x 41cm (8 x 16in) cream 28 count Meran fabric (DMC-E3972)

DMC stranded cotton (floss) as in chart key

Tapestry needle

Two pieces 4 x 19cm (1½ x 7⅛in) pink gingham fabric

Matching sewing thread

1m (40in) pink cord

1 Prepare your fabric for work (see Techniques). Fold the fabric in half to form a 20 x 20cm (8 x 8in) rectangle. Begin the design 5cm (2in) from the folded base, stitching over two fabric threads following the chart on page 103. Use two strands of stranded cotton (floss) for the cross stitch.

2 To make the bag, start with the design facing inwards, pin, tack (baste), then sew the two long side seams. Stitch a 1cm (½in) hem along the top edge. Remove any pins and tacking (basting) and then turn the bag right side out.

3 For the drawstring channel, press under a 6mm (¼in) hem along all four sides of both lengths of pink gingham. Centre a channel strip 2cm (¾in) from the top of the bag. Tack (baste) in place, then stitch along each long edge of the strip, leaving the short edges open to form the channel. Repeat with the other strip. To finish, thread the pink cord through the channel and knot the ends together.

STITCHING IDEAS

This little bag could also be used as a small gift sack filled with treats. The design would also look lovely in a nursery on the front of a tissue box or a nappy (diaper) holder.

Mr Bump Boot Bag

Mr Bump is the perfect choice for putting on the front of a boot bag. Only he could miss the football and lose his boot as well – he really must remember to tie his shoelaces up properly. If you have a favourite football team, you could use ribbon around the design in the colour of their strip.

STITCH COUNT

42 x 42

DESIGN SIZE

7.5 x 7.5cm (3 x 3in) approx

WHAT YOU NEED

16.5 x 19cm (6½ x 7½in) white 28 count Jobelan (Fabric Flair NJ249.00)

DMC stranded cotton (floss) as in chart key

Tapestry needle

75cm (30in) red ribbon

36 x 92cm (14 x 36in) blue gingham fabric

Matching sewing threads

●

1.3m (50in) white cord

1 Prepare your fabric for work and mark the centre (see Techniques). Begin stitching from the centre over two fabric threads following the chart on page 103. Use two strands of stranded cotton (floss) for cross stitching and one for backstitching.

2 To make up the boot bag, first bind the edges of the embroidered piece with the red ribbon, using matching sewing thread.

3 Take the gingham fabric and fold it in half so the short edges meet, arranging the fabric so the fold is at the bottom. With right sides together, pin, tack (baste) and then stitch the sides, matching the edges for a neat finish. Remove pins and tacking (basting).

4 Fold the top edge over to the wrong side by 6mm (¼in) and press. Fold the top edge over again 5cm (2in), to form the top of the bag. Pin in place and sew two rows of parallel stitching around the top to form a casing. Remove the pins and turn the bag to the right side. Snip the side seam between the lines of parallel stitching and bind the cut edges with buttonhole stitches or over-stitching.

5 Complete the bag by stitching the embroidery in the middle of the gingham, about 7.5cm (3in) from the fold. Finally, thread a length of white cord through the channel and secure the ends with knots.

STITCHING IDEAS

You could put this design on the front of a notebook used for keeping a record of your team's results. It would also look great on the front of a note block, pencil holder or paperweight.

Mr Men and Little Miss™& © 2002 Mrs Roger Hargreaves

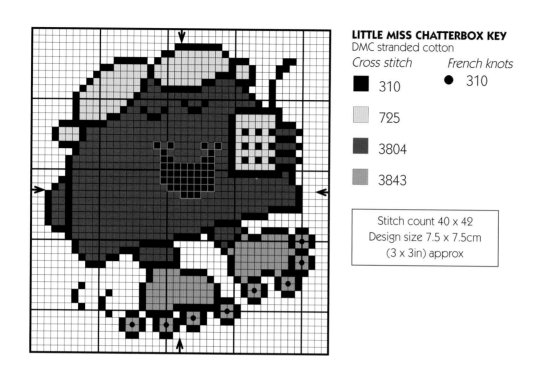

LITTLE MISS CHATTERBOX KEY
DMC stranded cotton

Cross stitch		French knots	
■	310	●	310
▨	725		
▨	3804		
▨	3843		

Stitch count 40 x 42
Design size 7.5 x 7.5cm
(3 x 3in) approx

LITTLE MISS SPLENDID KEY
DMC stranded cotton
Cross stitch

■	310	▨	907	⊡	B5200
■	666	▨	3843		
▨	725	▨	3850	*Backstitch*	
				——	310

Stitch count 31 x 42
Design size 5.5 x 7.5cm
(2¼ x 3in) approx

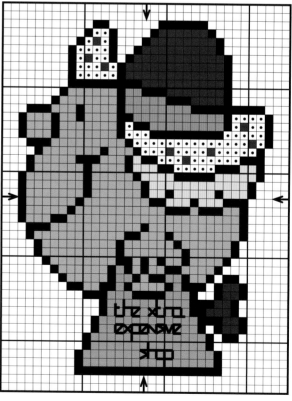

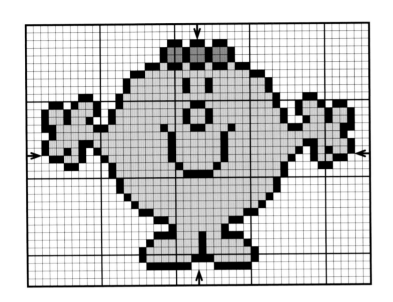

LITTLE MISS TINY KEY
DMC stranded cotton
Cross stitch

■ 310

▨ 604

▨ 3843

Stitch count 42 x 30
Design size 7.5 x 5.5cm
(3in x 2¼in) approx

MR BUMP KEY
DMC stranded cotton

Cross stitch   *Backstitch*

■ 310   —— 310

▨ 666

▨ 3843

• B5200

Stitch count 40 x 42
Design size 7.25 x 7.5cm
(2¾ x 3in) approx

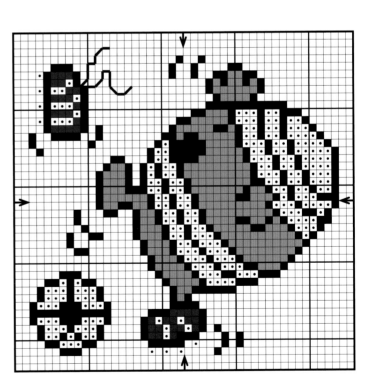

MR TICKLE KEY
DMC stranded cotton
Cross stitch

■ 310

▓ 3843

▒ 3853

Stitch count 42 x 42
Design size 7.5 x 7.5cm
(3 x 3in) approx

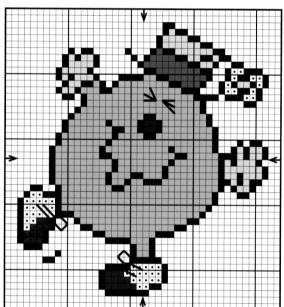

MR FUNNY KEY
DMC stranded cotton
Cross stitch

■ 310	▒ 725
▓ 666	▓ 825
▒ 704	• B5200

Backstitch
— 310

Stitch count 41 x 42
Design size 7.5 x 7.5cm
(3 x 3in) approx

MR STRONG KEY
DMC stranded cotton
Cross stitch

■ 310

▓ 666

▒ 976

▓ 911

• B5200

Stitch count 42 x 39
Design size 7.5 x 7cm
(2¾ x 3in) approx

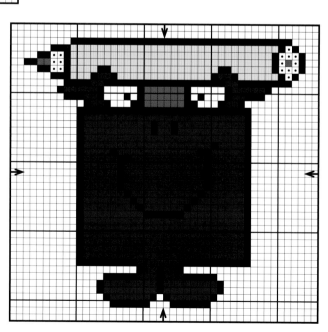

Mr Men and Little Miss™& © 2002 Mrs Roger Hargreaves

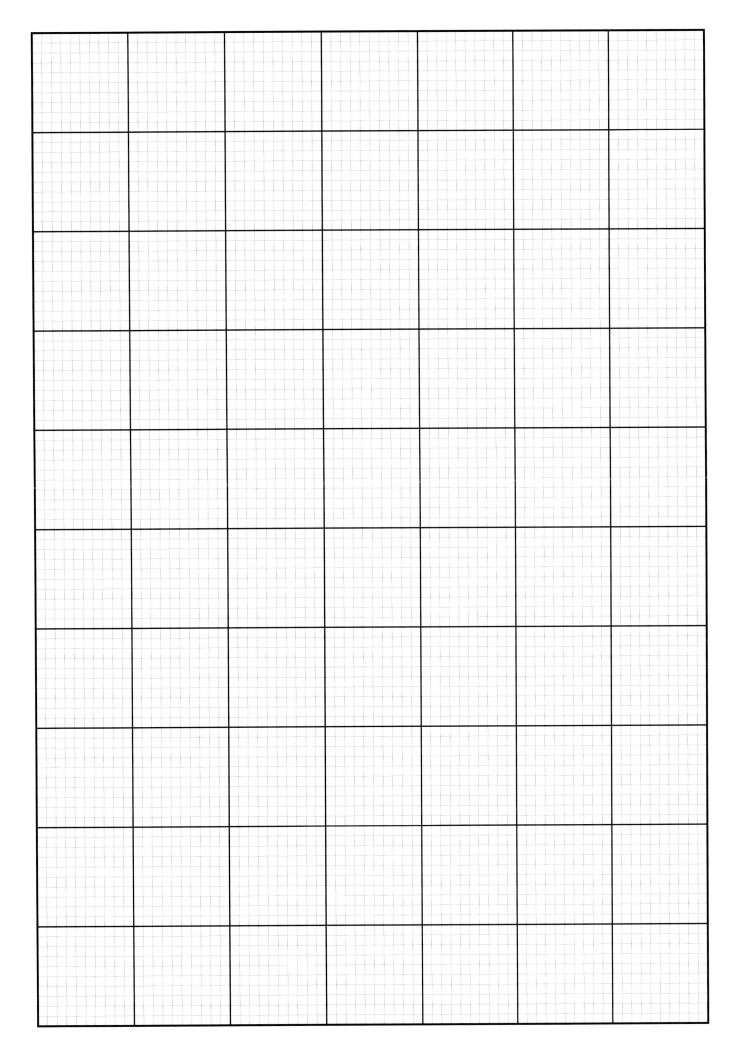

MATERIALS AND TECHNIQUES

This final section contains all you need to know about working the projects from this book: all the materials you will need, the stitches and techniques used in the designs and some handy tips for perfect work.

MATERIALS
Fabrics

There are many wonderful fabrics available today, in a vast array of colours and catering for many levels of ability. Fabrics used for counted cross stitch are all woven so they have the same number of threads or blocks to 2.5cm (1in), both horizontally and vertically. The two main fabric types used are block-weaves such as Aida, and evenweaves such as linen.

Blockweave Fabrics

These fabrics, commonly given the general name of Aida, are made of cotton and are woven in blocks making it very easy to count, as one cross stitch is worked over each block. There is a choice in the number of blocks per 2.5cm (1in), 14 count being the most commonly used. Aida is suitable for complete novices and comes in larger counts such as 12 and 8 which have only 12 and 8 holes per 2.5cm (1in), making theses useful for small children and the visually impaired.

Evenweave Fabrics

Linen is an evenweave fabric made from flax which has a natural slub, adding charm to the finished stitching. It is available in a large range of colours and types and is woven so that there is the same number of threads per 2.5cm (1in) horizontally and vertically, allowing the cross stitching to be of equal height and width.

Evenweaves come in a wide variety of thread counts; for example, a 28 count fabric has 28 threads to the 2.5cm (1in). As the stitching is usually worked over two threads, this produces 14 stitches to 2.5cm (1in). Therefore a design worked on 28 count evenweave will be the same size as when stitched on 14 count Aida.

Jobelan is the trade name for a range of colourful 28 count fabrics made from cotton and modal which makes it strong and easy to care for. It is particularly ideal where a practical application is required, for example for bags and sacks.

Waste Canvas

Waste canvas is a useful product readily available from needlework shops. It is designed for stitching on fabrics where cross stitch would not normally be possible because the threads are un-even, such as clothing. Simply tack (baste) a piece of waste canvas large enough for the design on to the chosen article and cross stitch the design through both fabrics. When all the stitching is complete, dampen the waste canvas and use tweezers to draw out the threads, leaving the design in place.

Threads

There is a vast choice of threads available. Those used predominantly in the book are DMC stranded cotton (floss), with colours and codes numbers given in the chart keys.

Stranded Cottons

The most commonly used thread for cross stitching is six-stranded mercerised cotton (floss) which has a lovely silk-like sheen. It is produced by several manufacturers and comes in a huge range of colours.

The strands in a skein are usually separated before starting to stitch – the number required for stitching depends on the count of the fabric you're stitching on. Generally two strands are used on 14 count fabrics and three strands on a bigger, more open weave such as 11 count. For finer work such as 22 count, one strand will give adequate coverage. Backstitches and long stitches generally use one strand.

Metallic Threads

Metallic threads are used to add a sparkle to a design. There are many varieties available and with experimentation you will find the thickness required for a particular count of fabric. Metallic threads feel different to stitch with and you will have to take more time to ensure that the threads sit in position well. Metallics tend to damage easily when passing through fabric and to prevent this it is advisable to use short lengths of no more than 45cm (18in) at a time. The moonscape duffel bag uses a silver metallic thread.

Flower Threads

This is a soft-textured, smooth thread with a matt finish, which can create quite a different look to a design. It is a single, non-divisible thread ideal for fine work and is available in a wide choice of colours. Danish Flower threads have been used to good effect on Shaun's Cushion.

Needles

A blunt tapestry needle is usually used for cross stitch. The most common sizes are No.24 for fabrics up to 14 count and No.26 for 16 count and finer. Be aware that nickel-plated needles will leave a mark on the fabric if left in it for any length of time. It is recommended that you take the needle out when leaving your work or alternately treat yourself to a wonderful gold needle, which will not tarnish.

Scissors

Sharp, fine-pointed embroidery scissors will be needed for cutting threads and also a pair of good, sharp dressmaking scissors for cutting fabric. Avoid using these for cutting paper or card because it will blunt them.

Hoops and Frames

It is a matter of personal preference whether you use a hoop or frame to house your stitching whilst working. Some feel that the fabric remains taut, making control of tension easier when using a hoop or frame, which may assist beginners. Others are concerned with the creasing of the fabric and the damage to the stitched that may occur. If you use a hoop, bind the edges of the frame with bias binding to prevent slippage and use tissue between the frames to prevent damage to the stitching. When you have finished working remove the fabric from the hoop to avoid excessive marks. There are many types of hoops and frames available – look in your local craft shop.

TECHNIQUES
Using charts

All the projects use counted cross stitch, with the designs worked from easy-to-read full-colour charts with keys. The arrows at the sides of each chart allow the centre point to be found easily. The charts are divided into a grid of squares, with the cross stitches indicating by coloured squares, which may also contain a symbol. So one square on the chart represents one stitch on the fabric. Blank squares on the chart mean that there is no stitching in that area. One stitch is over either one block of Aida or two threads of an evenweave fabric.

Some designs are outlined in backstitch and long stitch. These are shown by short or long coloured lines on the chart, and in places on many designs long stitches can be used to outline instead of backstitches. A long stitch is often used for grass stalks and animal whiskers. A French knot is shown by a coloured circle.

Calculating design size

Stitch counts and design sizes are given with all projects but if you wish to calculate this yourself, count the number of stitches horizontally and vertically on the chart. Divide each of these numbers by the number of stitches to 2.5cm (1in) on your fabric (i.e. the count) and this will give you the finished design size. You will then need to add an allowance to this for working the design and final mounting.

Fabric preparation

It is best to prepare your fabric before you start stitching. To prevent fraying, trim the edges of Aida fabric with pinking shears and for evenweaves overcast the edges either by hand or with zigzag stitching by machine.

It is preferable to work cross stitch from the centre of the design outwards, as this will ensure that the stitching is always central. To find the centre of the fabric fold it first in half and then into quarters. Lightly crease these folds and then mark the central lines with tacking (basting) stitches, which are removed when the work is complete. Match the central square on the chart with the central point on the chart.

THE STITCHES
Starting and finishing work

Do not use a knot to begin and end cross stitching as knots leave ugly bumps on the finished piece. Perhaps the simplest way to start is to make the first stitch and leave a 3cm (1¼in) long tail at the back of the fabric. This is then secured by working your first stitches over it.

To change thread or finish off, take the thread to the back of the work and pass it through a few adjacent stitches, away from the edges, for a neat finish.

Cross stitch

This is shown on charts by a coloured square, sometimes with a symbol. Cross stitch is usually worked with two strands of stranded cotton (floss). When working on Aida, cross stitches are worked diagonally over *one block*

between the holes (see Fig 1). When working on an evenweave such as linen, the cross stitches are worked over *two threads* of the fabric (see Fig 2).

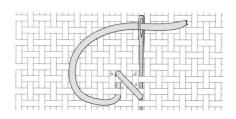

Fig 1   Fig 2

To work a whole cross stitch, follow Fig 3, bringing the needle up from the back of the fabric to the front at (a). Cross diagonally and go down to the back at (b) and come up again at (c). Cross diagonally and go down at (d) to finish the stitch. One golden rule is that the top diagonal stitch should always be in the same direction.

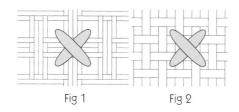

Fig 3

When covering large areas you may prefer to work cross stitch in rows. To do this, work the first half of a row of

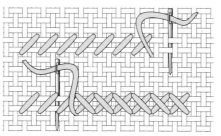

Fig 4

cross stitches and then return along the row, completing the cross stitches (see Fig 4).

Three-quarter cross stitch

Three-quarter cross stitch is used to give more detail to a design. It is shown on charts by a coloured triangle in one half of a square. Work the first half of a cross stitch, then work the second stitch diagonally but take the needle down through the centre hole, or pierce the fabric if working on Aida (see Fig 5)

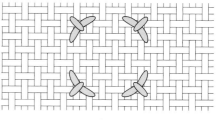

Fig 5

Backstitch

Backstitch is used for outlining a design or defining some parts of it. It is indicated by short coloured lines on the charts and usually uses one strand of stranded cotton (floss).

Following Fig 6, bring the needle to the front, one block (or two evenweave threads) ahead of the starting point.

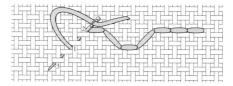

Fig 6

Make a stitch back to the starting point, then re-emerge one block (or two evenweave threads) ahead of the last completed stitch.

Long stitch

Long stitches are used when a longer stitch than a backstitch is required, or for quicker outlining results (Fig 7). They are shown on the charts by a long coloured line. Use one strand of stranded cotton (floss) unless otherwise instructed.

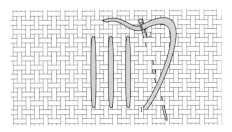

Fig 7

French knots

French knots are a useful accompaniment to cross stitch and usually use one strand of stranded cotton (floss). To work a French knot, bring the needle up to the front of the fabric and wrap the thread twice around the needle, as shown in Fig 8. Still holding the thread, return the needle through the fabric one thread or part of a block away, pulling the thread gently to form a loose knot.

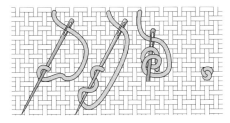

Fig 8

Ten tips for perfect stitching

● Use a good pair of embroidery scissors with sharp points – essential for ease of working and for a neat finish.

● Use a length of thread no more than 18in (46cm) long in order to prevent tangles.

● All the top diagonal stitches in cross stitch should lie in the same direction for a neat finish.

● Do not pull the stitches too tightly, they should sit 'graciously' on the fabric.

● Drop your needle every now and then and let it spin, this will take the twists out and so avoiding infuriating tangles.

● Do not carry threads across an open expanse of fabric: finish off and begin again. Loose threads, particularly dark ones, will be visible from the right side when the work is complete.

● When working on dark fabrics it is hard to see the holes. Use a white pillowcase or similar over your knee and the holes will show up more clearly.

● Look after your eyes by using a daylight bulb for night-time stitching, a magnifier when the fabric is fine and take regular breaks, every twenty minutes or so, to rest and readapt your vision. The benefit is fewer mistakes.

● If you are using several small designs to make up a larger picture, plan the whole design before you begin stitching. Photocopy the charts, cut out the shapes and position them on a large piece of graph paper and use this as your guide.

● Don't leave needles in fabric or fabric in hoops for any length of time, to avoid marking and creasing your work.

Bibliography

BARKLEM, Jill *Spring Story* (HarperCollins, 1980)
BARKLEM, Jill *Summer Story* (HarperCollins, 1980)
BARKLEM, Jill *Autumn Story* (HarperCollins, 1980)
BARKLEM, Jill *Winter Story* (HarperCollins, 1980)

BUTTERWORTH, Nick *After the Storm* (HarperCollins, 1992)
BUTTERWORTH, Nick *The Secret Path* (HarperCollins, 1994)
BUTTERWORTH, Nick *A Bumpy Ride* (HarperCollins, 1999)

HARGREAVES, Roger *Mr Men* and *Little Miss* series (Price Stern Sloan Inc., 1981)

MURPHY, Jill *Five Minutes' Peace* (Walker Books, 1986)
MURPHY, Jill *All in One Piece* (Walker Books, 1987)
MURPHY, Jill *A Piece of Cake* (Walker Books, 1989)
MURPHY, Jill *A Quiet Night In* (Walker Books, 1993)
MURPHY, Jill *The Large Family Collection* (Walker Books, 2000)

WHYBROW, Ian & REYNOLDS, Adrian *Harry and the Snow King* (Levinson, 1997)
WHYBROW, Ian & REYNOLDS, Adrian *Harry and the Bucketful of Dinosaurs* (David & Charles Children's Books, 1999)
WHYBROW, Ian & REYNOLDS, Adrian *Harry and the Robot* (David & Charles Children's Books, 2000)
WHYBROW, Ian & REYNOLDS, Adrian *Harry and the Dinosaurs Say 'Raah!'* (Gullane Children's Books, 2001)
Reproduced by kind permission of Gullane Children's Books

Suppliers

Card Art
14 Kensington Industrial Park, Hall Street, Southport,
Merseyside, PR9 0NY.
Tel: 01704 549754
For a comprehensive range of aperture cards

DMC Creative World
Pullman Road, Wigston, Leicester, LE18 2DY.
Tel: 0116 281 1040   Fax: 0116 281 3592
Website: www.dmc/cw.com

DMC Needlecraft Pty,
51-66 Carrington Road
Marrickville, NSW 2204, Australia

DMC Corporation
Port Kearney Blvd No 10
South Kearney, NJ 070732-0650
*For stranded cottons, metallic threads, Aida and evenweave
fabrics and a wide range of embroidery supplies*

Fabric Flair Ltd
Unit 3 Northlands Industrial Estate, Copheap Lane,
Warminster, Wiltshire, BA12 0BG.
Tel: 01985 846845
For Aida and Jobelan fabrics

Framecraft Miniatures Ltd
372–376 Summer Lane,
Hockley, Birmingham,
B19 3QA.
Tel: 0121 2120551   Fax: 0121 212 0552
Website: www.framecraft.com

Gay Bowles Sales Inc, PO Box 1060
Janesville WI, USA

Ireland Needlecraft Pty Ltd
2-4 Keppel Drive
Hallam, Victoria 3803, Australia
*For pencil pots, ceramic pots, rulers, fun clips and mugs, plus
other products suitable for displaying embroidery*

Little Boxes
5 South Marlow Street, Hadfield, Derbyshire,
SK13 2AL.
For pine boxes

Adele Welsby Designs
Church House, St Mary Church, Cowbridge,
Vale of Glamorgan, CF71 7LT.
Tel/Fax: 01446 773029
For Percy the Park Keeper cross stitch kits

Acknowledgments

Thank you to the following people who made extremely valuable contributions to this project.

John, Matthew and Laura, for their support and tolerance over many months and particularly towards the end when juggling projects became an art form.

Dotti, for never complaining no matter how tight the deadline even when celebrating very special birthdays and anniversaries. Hil (Kingfisher Gallery), for her excellent framing.

Lin, a very special thank you for rescuing me many times. This book would not have been completed without your help, advice and calming influence.

Cheryl, Ali, Lisa, Sandra and the rest of the team at David and Charles, for all their support and encouragement.

Last but not least, all the contributors and suppliers for all their help, advice and supplies, so necessary in the creation of this book.

Index

Illustrations shown in *italic*; charts shown in **bold**